PERCY THROWER'S GUIDE TO
COLOUR IN YOUR GARDEN

Do most of us appreciate the importance of colour in our gardens? Superficially the answer may be Yes, but more fundamentally it is probably No, despite the fact that colour and its intelligent use to form pleasing plant associations and contrasts is one of the aspects of gardening which make it an endlessly fascinating pastime. For the colour-conscious gardener the planning of planting schemes has a very special exhilaration, and the advice which *Percy Thrower's Guide to Colour in Your Garden* gives opens up endless possibilities for the resourceful gardener.

Percy Thrower, with his unrivalled knowledge of practical gardening, puts the position in a nutshell when he says: 'Much has been said about the design of gardens, and many plans have been published for the guidance of those who wish to make or remodel a garden. In all this advice astonishingly little attention has been paid to the correct use of colour in the garden, yet colour is the most important attribute of many popular flowers'. Now, in this book, we find the answers to many of our problems.

Naturally, the use of colour in any garden depends primarily on the owner's personal taste and interest. This could not be otherwise. What Percy Thrower sets out to do is to provide an understanding of the broad principles which should guide one in respect of colour when considering planting schemes or, indeed, laying out a garden, and to follow this with suggestions on a wide range of plants which could contribute in one way or another to this aspect of gardening. *Percy Thrower's Guide to Colour in Your Garden* is a source of ideas and it points the way clearly to more adventurous gardening.

OTHER BOOKS BY PERCY THROWER

PERCY THROWER'S GUIDE TO
Colour in Your
GARDEN

*

Best Wishes

Percy Thrower

Cape Town Oct 1968

W. H. & L. COLLINGRIDGE LTD · LONDON

First published in 1966
by W. H. & L. Collingridge Ltd
Tower House, Southampton Street, W.C.2
Filmset by Photoprint Plates Limited
Wickford, Essex
Printed in the Netherlands by
Grafische Industrie N.V. Haarlem
© W. H. & L. Collingridge 1966

Contents

ACKNOWLEDGEMENTS

I would like to thank *Amateur Gardening* for providing most of the photographs reproduced in this book, and the following photographers who have also contributed: Miss Valerie Finnis, Mr A. J. Huxley, Mr D. Merrett, Mr R. V. G. Rundle, Mr H. Smith and Mr A. Starkey.

PERCY THROWER

CHAPTER ONE

Colour in Perspective

MUCH has been said about the design of gardens, and many plans have been published for the guidance of those who wish to make or remodel gardens. In all this advice astonishingly little attention has been paid to the correct use of colour in the garden, yet colour is the most important attribute of many popular flowers.

Our sense of colour is a very personal matter. In some people it is highly developed, others scarcely have it at all. We say of these that they are colour blind, or at any rate blind to some colours, and this is a much more common defect than many people imagine. Partial colour blindness probably accounts for some of the more violent disagreements that occur regarding the correct use, and in particular the correct association, of colours but I am sure they depend also upon much more subtle differences in our individual make up.

For all these reasons it would be foolish for me to be too dogmatic about the use of colour in the garden, for what I like others may dislike. Yet I find that people constantly seek for guidance on this matter just as they seek for guidance in the use of colour in the home, and I think that many of the same principles apply in both garden and home. One can learn a lot by studying what the best home decorators recommend; the colours they are prepared to put together and those they are at pains to keep apart. One can learn, too, from their use of various textures, for texture also enters into the pattern of the garden.

The Colour Wheel

Colours can be considered quite scientifically and objectively in relation to the spectrum. At one extreme are the various shades of red, at the other those of blue and violet, with orange, yellow and green linking them together. There is a device know as a colour wheel (see p. 18) in which the major colours are represented in a circle. The usefulness of this wheel is that it shows, at a glance, which colours can be associated and what the broad effect will be. Colours on opposite sides of the wheel will give strong contrasts. Neighbouring colours on the wheel will give blending effects.

Of course, the colour wheel is quite a crude and simple device. It really only allows for the simplest colours, and makes no provision for the multitude of shades and tints which one finds in plants and upon the clever use of which some of the most delightful colour effects depend. But

[7]

This border of annuals (shown in colour on p. 48) illustrates how a pattern depending on colour loses its force in monochrome

at least it provides some basic facts for those who do not feel very inventive regarding the handling of colour.

What Does Colour Do?

I think it is just as well to get quite clear in one's mind what purposes colour serves in the garden. As I see it these can all be classified under two headings, and they really have little or nothing to do with one another. Colour may be used to form patterns and it may be used to create moods.

Of course, pattern making in gardens depends upon many other things than colour. Primarily I think it should depend on form; on the shape of beds and borders, the lines created by paths and walls, and the silhouettes of plants, particularly of the more permanent plants such as trees and shrubs.

When the pattern making in a garden depends too heavily upon colour and too little on these dimensional characteristics the weakness is revealed in any monochrome photograph. The garden, which to the eye or in a colour photograph was full of interest, disintegrates and becomes a shapeless mess. We have all seen a good many gardens like that.

Another weakness in the garden that relies too much on colour for its pattern making is that it tends to hold its pattern for too short a period each year. For one of the major difficulties with plant colour, and, incidentally, a major difference between colour in the garden and colour in the home, is that it does not last. Flowers fade, some of them all too quickly, and even foliage changes its hue with the season. So while the home maker can plan in paints and fabrics which are going to look much the same from January to December, the garden maker must work with materials that are changing all the time. It is all very exciting but it can be a bit puzzling and even, at times, exasperating.

So much, then, for pattern making with colours. Now what about the creation of moods? Here we enter the realm of subjectivity with a vengeance, for what creates delight in one person quite often creates fury in another. Yet even here I think some general principles can be laid down.

Cold Colours and Hot Colours

Blue, for example, is a cool colour (some would even go so far as to say that it is positively cold). When we are a little depressed we say that we 'have a fit of the blues' and though I certainly do not regard blue in the garden as depressing it has a quietening effect.

By contrast, red and orange are hot colours. They tend to excite rather than to quiet the mind, and they excite some

[8]

In this border the sword-like yuccas, large-leaved rheum and the bold sweep of flat-headed Sedum spectabile *provide striking contrasts of form and thus are effective in monochrome as well as in colour. Such a border retains its interest for much longer than one relying entirely on colour*

people so much that they simply cannot stand them.

Many pinks are restful but this is not true of all shades of pink, certainly not of those that contain a fair amount of blue and which I refer to in more general terms as puce or magenta. These can be extremely harsh to the eye, and unless carefully placed in the garden they can result in frightful colour clashes offensive to most eyes.

Yellows are of so many different qualities that it is difficult to generalise about them, but the stronger yellows certainly tend to liven up the garden picture. But again one has to handle them with care for in bad company they can produce some harsh effects.

Some people say they do not like white flowers but I think they are quite indispensable in the garden. A few well-placed whites in a border will liven up all the other colours without creating any offensive clashes of their own. Together with silver, white is one of the most useful ingredients in the garden maker's palette for breaking the dominance of the strong colours without losing any of their overall brilliance.

The Importance of Green
Green is a different matter altogether. It is the most useful of all the garden colours because it will harmonise with them all and tone down the harshness of the most aggressive. But, unlike white, it does lower

[9]

the general level of brilliance. Again a monochrome photograph can be very revealing of what I am trying to express. Take such a picture of a garden in which there are a lot of white flowers and the result will certainly be lively whatever else it may be. Take another photograph of a garden in which green predominates and the result may be soft and hazy to the point of dullness.

But never underestimate the importance of green. If you look at floral decorations today you cannot fail to note the popularity of combinations of green and yellow, pale yellows in particular, and lime green. Do not forget that there are all sorts of green just as there are all sorts of red, blue, yellow and all the other colours. If you want something really charming and restful and a little different, you might even consider planning some part of the garden entirely in shades of green.

Where Colours can be Used Freely

There are some gardens, and some places in the garden, where colour can be used more freely than in others. Bedding-out schemes are usually conceived in terms of massed colour and often for quite contrary reasons. In very small gardens or in formal town gardens cheerful bedding-out plants provide the best way of giving gaiety to what might otherwise be a rather dull picture, and as they must be changed with the seasons, the picture itself is a changing one. In a big garden one could contrive such changes by placing plants of different seasons near to one another so that, as the flowers of one fade, the flowers of another

Colour can often be used freely in small town gardens as the aim is to brighten rather dull surroundings. Scarlet salvias dominate the centre of the garden and the backcloth of Bilderdyckia (Polygonum) balds-chuanicum, *the vigorous Russian Vine, screens a brick wall. The geraniums provide colour at a different level*

open, but that is not possible unless there is plenty of space.

Bedding-out plants are also very appropriate in public parks because there one is out to make the maximum effect. It is like an orchestra playing crescendo; it is all very exciting and fine so long as one has not got to stay with it too long—and public parks are places to visit rather than to live in. Incidentally, the cost, in terms of plants and labour and resources, such as frames and greenhouses, for maintaining that crescendo of colour, would be quite beyond most amateur gardeners.

Colour can be laid on heavily in the herbaceous border, too, and this was the traditional way of doing things, with the plants in bold groups of a kind. This kind of planting is still carried out in some large gardens and public parks, but it is not, in my opinion, the best way to handle herbaceous plants in ordinary gardens, mainly because there is not the space to get these bold effects. Even if one does, by hook or by crook, contrive them they tend to be short lived. Not many herbaceous perennials flower for more than four or five weeks at a time, and so considerable ingenuity in grouping is necessary if the display of the herbaceous border is to be continuous for several months. Of course, one can overcome this to some extent by mixing temporary plants—bedding plants and annuals and dahlias—with the herbaceous plants, but there is a limit to what can be achieved in an average private garden.

In such places I think it is better to plant herbaceous perennials in ones and twos, or at most in groups of three, and not to worry at all if there are considerable stretches of green where plants have already flowered or are yet to come into flower. Such a border cannot compare with more colourful ones for sheer excitment, but it

In this tiny town yard, pot-grown geraniums, a rambler rose in a built-up border and colourful garden furniture create an air of gaiety

is much more restful and, if I may use the phrase, 'liveable with'.

Tree and Shrub Colour

All this is even more true of tree and shrub colour. Some of the very large gardens contrive quite fantastic colour displays with rhododendrons and azaleas, but usually such gardens tend to be colourful for a brief period only. They have their heyday in May and are pretty dull for the rest of the year, though some contrive a second burst of colour with hydrangeas in summer.

This brings to my mind a rather unusual rhododendron garden planned by an amateur who is very sensitive to colour. It is conceived entirely in shades of blue and yellow with occasional white to liven things up. Nothing clse obtrudes at this particular season though other colour effects, not dependent upon rhododendrons, appear at other times of the year. This kind of planning requires great fore-thought and considerable knowledge of the precise colours and flowering times, and the heights and rates of growth of plants, but it can be immense fun and is well worth doing if one has the time and the inclination.

Rhododendron and azalea colour can be rather hot and tiring, as any reader who visits a garden where these splendid shrubs are planted widely and in a conventional way will see for himself. One must be especially careful about colour groupings, too, for a colour like bluey-pink—which is found in azaleas—can be an intrusion when seen against a background of, say, coppery-orange.

By using marked discs, preferably in the colour of the plants represented, it is possible to avoid colour disharmonies when planning a border on paper

How To Make a Plan

There are many ways of approaching the problem of preparing colour schemes for one's own garden. Some people do a lot of preliminary paper work and some do not. I am in the latter category but then I have had a good many years at the game. It is not difficult for me to visualise the colours, heights and shapes of the various plants and to bear in mind their respective seasons of beauty. I build up schemes in my mind's eye and then I go out and turn them into reality in the garden. I do not carry out a great deal of formal planning on paper, though for future reference I make notes of schemes I have liked in my own garden, or in gardens I have visited or seen in pictures.

I fancy most amateur gardeners, and particularly beginners, will find it easier to do a bit more paper work before they ac-tually set to work in the garden. One simple and effective way of doing this is to draw a fairly large outline plan to scale of the borders or beds you wish to plant and then, on separate slips of paper or cardboard, write down the names of the plants you fancy. There should be one strip (in practice it may be better to make it an oval or a circle) for each plant or group of plants of the same variety. In addition to the name, write down on this slip of paper the height of the plant, its flowering season and its colour or, better still, if you want to be really thorough, put a splash of the colour on the slip with a paint brush.

Then you can arrange your slips on your outline plan, rather like putting a jig-saw puzzle together. You can see just how the colours are going to come together. It will be possible to check that colours meant to coincide in time really will do so, for many an otherwise excellent scheme has gone awry simply through neglect of this ele-mentary matter. You will also be able to make sure that a tall plant will not hide the display of a short one, but if possible will provide an effective background to it. Of course, it does not so much matter in a herbaceous border if an earlier flowering 'shorty' is later screened by a later flowering plant of greater height; indeed sometimes this can be the most effective means of masking what might otherwise be ugly blanks in the borders.

Viewpoints from the House

All planning schemes should be con-

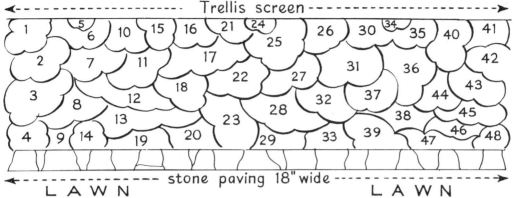

Plants in this 8-ft.-wide herbaceous border, designed for an all-summer display, are: 1, Achillea fili-pendulina *Gold Plate.* 2, Cimicifuga *White Pearl.* 3, *Lupin Russell Hybrids.* 4, Aster amellus *King George.* 5, *Climbing rose Albertine.* 6, Delphinium *Blackmore's Glorious.* 7, Aster *Crimson Brocade.* 8, Achillea taygetea. 9, Heuchera *Lady Romney.* 10, Sidalcea *Crimson Beauty.* 11, Phlox *Duchess of York.* 12, *Hemerocallis (orange).* 13, Erigeron *Festivity.* 14, Armeria *Bee's Ruby.* 15, Aster *The Archbishop.* 16, Thalictrum glaucum. 17, *Lupin Russell Hybrids.* 18, Chrysanthemum maximum *Esther Read.* 19, Sedum spectabile. 20, Dianthus *Mrs Sinkins.* 21, Aconitum wilsonii *Kelmscott.* 22, Knipho-fia uvaria. 23, Salvia superba *Lubeca.* 24, *Climbing rose Danse du Feu.* 25, Delphinium *Blue Jade.* 26, Aster *Marie Ballard.* 27, Anthemis *Grallagh Gold.* 28, Astilbe *Fanal.* 29, Trollius *Commander-in-Chief.* 30, Campanula lactiflora *Prichard's Variety.* 31, Phlox *Mrs Ethel Prichard.* 32, Gaillardia *Mrs Longster.* 33, Physostegia *Vivid.* 34, *Climbing rose Golden Showers.* 35, Helianthus *Lodden Gold.* 36, Helenium *Wyndley.* 37, Paeonia lobata *Sunshine.* 38, Achillea *The Pearl.* 39, Nepeta *Six Hills Giant.* 40, Delphinium *Royalist.* 41, Heliopsis *Golden Plume.* 42, Aster *Pat Ballard.* 43, Aster *Blue Radiance.* 44, Papaver *Mrs Perry.* 45, Solidago *Leda.* 46, Veronica subsessilis hendersonii. 47, Dianthus *Doreen.* 48, Santolina incana

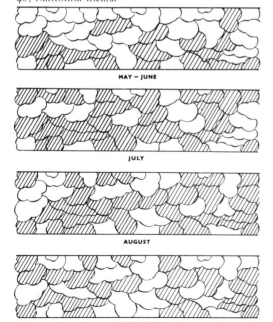

sidered from the viewpoint from which they will be seen most frequently. In small gardens this is more often than not the house and it will pay to make frequent visits to this and survey the garden from the principal windows, trying to visualise just what the schemes you are planning will look like from these. Do not forget the kitchen window, for it may well be the room in which your wife spends a good part of each day and she deserves a pleasant outlook.

The Dingle in Quarry Park, Shrewsbury, which has been in my charge now for many years, is particularly difficult to colour-plan because it can be looked at

The four flowering charts (left) refer to the plan at the head of this page. The shaded areas indicate when the plants will be in flower

from all sides and in many places from above too. You get things right from one viewpoint only to discover that they are hopelessly wrong from another. This is the kind of problem that only gets solved by experience, by trying one arrangement and then another until eventually everything falls into place according to your liking.

Woodland, Stream-side and Rock Gardens

I think colour needs to be used fairly sparingly in the woodland garden and by pool and stream-side. These should all be cool and restful places not overburdened with hot and tiring colour. A woodland path with azaleas lining it on one side can be a really lovely scene, a study in pink and mauve with plenty of green to set it off. Put a strong yellow into that and you would kill it completely.

Stream-side gardens should always be planted with an eye to form as well as colour. For example, to provide interest in the middle distance such plants as the giant cow parsnip or heracleum can be used, provided the scale of this planting is appropriate to their size. This has flat heads of white flowers and good leaves as well as a rather statuesque form, and it sits in well with low-growing primulas and other small plants along the side of a stream. One should avoid strong colour contrasts which would destroy the peace of the picture.

Rock gardens need quite a lot of thought. They can so easily be a bit gaudy and brash in spring and then rather dull for the rest of the year. Generally the colours want to be well mixed and spread over as long a season as possible. Too much purple aubrieta and yellow alyssum can upset the balance, though I am a great admirer of both flowers and like to see the deep yellow and pale alyssums planted together for colour harmony.

Planting Walls

Then there is the problem of planting walls. Stone walls and weathered timber seldom present much difficulty for if they are in some shade of grey, as they usually are, that is a neutral colour which will go with anything. But brick can be difficult and the redder it is the greater the difficulty so far as colour planning is concerned. I made a mistake when I planted the scarlet firethorn, *Pyracantha coccinea lalandii*, on the wall of my house in Quarry Park. Fortunately it has grown so fast that you do not see much of the brick which otherwise would clash in colour with the orange-red berries.

Honeysuckles go with red brick and so does the winter jasmine. One has to be careful with roses, particularly pink and red roses, but the yellows, buffs and whites should be all right.

The Special Problem of Red

I have already referred to the special problem of red in any part of the garden. Someone has said that reds burn holes in the landscape and I know exactly what they mean. So many reds simply do not blend in well and the eye treats them as something extraneous to the rest. That very popular, but I think overrated, rose Super Star is a case in point. Personally I will not plant it, but a lot of people like it. They can put it right by itself surrounded by green or they can associate it with white or some of the softer yellows and buffs. But it is not at all easy to get it really into the picture.

In summer bedding scarlet salvia is much more difficult than red geranium simply because it produces so much bloom that practically none of its own foliage remains to be seen. Even the best of the red geraniums retain plenty of visible green leaves throughout the height of their flowering season. I always use plenty of silver foliage along with the red in all my summer colour schemes. *Centaurea gymnocarpa* and *Cineraria maritima* (or, to give it its most up-to-date name, *Senecio cineraria*) are invaluable silvers, and I also bring in soft golden-yellow in the plant known as Golden Feather which is, in fact, *Chrysanthemum parthenium aureum,* sometimes catalogued as *Matricaria eximia aurea.*

Bark and Foliage Effects

In winter one can take all the colour one can get and there is never really enough of it. Some of the bark effects can be very lovely, the yellows of some of the willows, the reds of the dogwood and the grey or blue-whites of the whitewash brambles. These are all colours which light up beautifully in the winter sun.

In winter, too, evergreen shrubs come into their own. For this reason evergreens should be placed very carefully in mixed plantations and shrubberies. Remember that you are planning here for two totally different pictures. In summer, when all the shrubs are in leaf, all will merge in together but in winter, when the deciduous shrubs are bare skeletons, the evergreens will stand out alone. They must be placed so that they look right then and make an entirely new grouping of their own.

Foliage plants of all kinds, herbaceous as well as shrubby, can be tremendously important in giving firmness and permanence to the scenes one is attempting to create. Some herbaceous plants have an almost architectural or sculptured appearance, the hostas, rodgersias, and acanthus more so than any others, I think. Their leaves are large and well formed, and the colours are pleasing and harmonise with almost anything else one wants to use. There is plenty of colour variation in hostas, too, grey, blue and green, as well as silver and gold variegated varieties which can be very effective indeed.

Colour in Spring

One thing you have to remember when composing any early spring picture for the garden is that, apart from a few evergreens, there will be no green from the trees. They will be bare and so any green you need must come from the grass or from the foliage of the plants themselves. That is one reason why I prefer some of the wild tulips and the hybrids from wild tulips such as the Water Lily tulips (*Tulipa kaufmanniana* and its varieties) and Peacock tulips (*T. greigii* and its varieties) to the Darwin and Cottage tulips because many of them have quite decorative and interesting leaves, often striped with maroon or chocolate.

Many people like what are called garden tulips but I find them rather difficult to place. They are too stiff and set for my liking, especially when planted in blocks of colour as they usually are. Personally, I plant them individually or in small groups here and there for a touch of colour.

Just as I find a personal difficulty with the conventional massed tulips, so do I have difficulty in reconciling myself to wallflowers massed to colour. Broadly we have seven basic colours to work with, the blood red, fiery red, orange, deep yellow, pale yellow, purple and the Eastern Queen type of rose. I have never been able to separate these to my liking, and so I generally plant orange, yellow and blood red all mixed together and this seems to me to be an eye catcher.

Another point in spring bedding where I find myself at variance with general practice is in the use of edgings. For summer there is plenty of choice of good edging plants. One can use a compact lobelia or alyssum, *Centaurea candidissima,* or the Golden Feather (*Chrysanthemum*

Even a small pool introduces a new element to the garden—the reflection of the sky, clouds and near-by plants in still water

other places the almond and grape hyacinth combination might be the one to go for.

In May and early June we get the lovely and in many instances quite unique colours of the bearded irises. They all blend together admirably, but you need enough of the brighter blues and the whites and yellows to liven up some of the more sombre purple, mulberry and smoky violet shades. Irises will go along with other flowers in the herbaceous borders, but the most beautiful effects I have seen with them have always been in iris gardens, or even quite small iris beds which they occupy more or less in isolation.

Water as a Mirror

So far I have said nothing about water in the garden except in so far as it was implied in my comments about the streamside garden. But that was running water. Still water is quite another thing for, provided it is reasonably clear, it introduces an entirely new element to the garden—reflection. Water is to the garden as a mirror is to a room. It increases its apparent size and at the same time captivates the eye with new angles on familiar scenes. Water in the garden even captures the sky and brings it down to earth, for on a clear day the pool will be blue and on a dull day it will be grey. If there are billowing white clouds up above you will have the whiteness added to the picture you have composed in your garden.

This is what nature gives you immediately you introduce still, clear water to your garden. Art and artifice can give you more. Plants and ornaments and even garden furniture can be placed so that their images, too, are captured in the still surface of the pool.

parthenium aureum) to which I have already referred, and any of these can easily be kept neat and tidy. But for spring there is no such choice. Forget-me-not is too loose unless you are fortunate enough to get a really good strain. Polyanthus makes a poor edging though it is magnificent occupying a bed on its own. Arabis cannot be relied upon so I always take the polyanthus or the wallflowers right out to the edge of the bed.

Colour Combinations

One spring combination that always looks lovely is grape hyacinth planted under pink almond or cherry. Actually, with me, the almond flowers a bit too early for the grape hyacinth and a Japanese cherry such as Kanzan or Shirofugen is just right, but in

If polyanthus are the epitome of spring then delphiniums, so glorious in their modern forms, may fairly be considered the aristocrats of summer flowers. The cool beauty of their colours, from purple, through shades of blue to lilac-pink and white, is like a breath of fresh air on balmy summer days. Here, delphiniums have a perfect accompaniment in a philadelphus

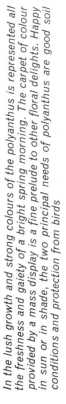

In the lush growth and strong colours of the polyanthus is represented all the freshness and gaiety of a bright spring morning. The carpet of colour provided by a mass display is a fine prelude to other floral delights. Happy in sun or in shade, the two principal needs of polyanthus are good soil conditions and protection from birds

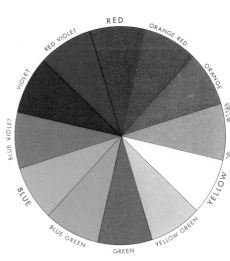

Above: Adjacent colours on the wheel harmonise with one another, whereas those on opposite sides of the wheel contrast strongly

The foliage of many trees and shrubs provide rich colours in autumn which add much to the garden scene. Here, in the lovely garden at Abbotswood, Stow-on-the-Wold, Gloucestershire, Japanese maples lead the eye to more subtle sylvan pleasures

The cold embrace of winter relaxes in the warm glow of Salix vitellina britzensis, one of the finest of all willows for coloured stems. As the best colour is provided by young bark, hard pruning in March is advisable to encourage new growth

CHAPTER TWO

Growing Plants for Short-term Display

IT COULD be said that all ornamental plants are grown in gardens for display, for they are certainly there to be looked at, and most gardeners will want to place them and grow them so that they look their best. Here I am concerned with a rather special aspect of gardening for display—the cultivation of plants that are intended to maintain colour for a while, and then be removed to make way for other plants that will keep up the display as continuously and effectively as possible. This kind of gardening is immensely important in public parks and is quite practicable in small gardens, too, because the numbers of plants required will not be great and many of them can be raised at home.

The plants required for display gardening can be broadly divided into those that are raised annually from seed (they are not all annuals), and those that are raised from cuttings or divisions. The seed plants can themselves be sub-divided into those that need to be raised under glass and those that can be sown out of doors, but there is no sharp dividing line between the two as much depends on locality and time of sowing.

Raising half-hardy perennials and half-hardy annuals from seed. Left : The compost in a seed box is made level and firm with a wooden presser. Right : The seeds are then sprinkled thinly and evenly over the surface of the compost

Left : Very small seeds do not need covering but others should be covered with a thin layer of the same compost mixture as that already used, this being scattered through a sieve. Right : The contents of the seed box are then thoroughly watered from a can fitted with a fine rose

HALF-HARDY PERENNIALS FROM SEED

I will take these first because most of them need to be sown first. Under this heading come the tuberous-rooted begonias which are rapidly increasing in popularity, sweet-smelling heliotrope, many verbenas (though I raise two of my special favourites, Lawrence Johnston and Loveliness, from cuttings), dwarf bedding dahlias, and lobelia, the scarlet salvia (now available in other colours), the fibrous rooted begonias and antirrhinums—though most gardeners think of them and treat them as annuals. All these plants need to be sown in March; in fact if a temperature of 16° to 18°C. (60° to 65°F.) can be maintained with fair certainty, it is worth sowing the antirrhinums, begonias and salvias in the latter half of February, as bigger plants will be

Left : After the seed box has been watered it is covered with a sheet of newspaper—and a sheet of glass underneath this if so desired—until germination takes place. Right : A week to ten days after germination the seedlings are pricked out into other boxes

obtained by this means. But it is necessary to think ahead and remember that it will be unsafe to plant outdoors until late May except in some very mild seaside places, and that plants from February sowings, if they have grown well, will almost certainly need to be grown individually in small pots for the last few weeks before they go out. At this stage 40 or 50 plants can take up quite a lot of room so it is no use sowing very early if this space, under protection of some kind, is not going to be available.

In theory all these half-hardy perennials could be kept from year to year; in practice it is seldom worth while to perpetuate any of them except the tuberous-rooted begonias, which can be stored dry during the winter in a frost-proof cupboard, and so will present no problems at a time when greenhouse space will almost certainly be needed for other things. The rest can be raised so easily and cheaply each year from seed that this is the simplest course to adopt.

HALF-HARDY ANNUALS

Under this heading are included a great many of the most popular summer bedding plants: ageratum, asters, arctotis, Giant Chabaud carnations, cleome, cosmos, *Dianthus heddewigii*, matricaria, French and African marigolds, *Mesembryanthemum criniflorum*, nemesia, nicotiana, petunia, portulaca, *Phlox drummondii,* annual rudbeckia, stocks, *Tagetes signata,* ursinia, venidium and zinnia. It is an impressive list and of some kinds, notably the asters, marigolds, petunias and zinnias, there are innumerable varieties so that there really is something for every place and every need.

RAISING HALF-HARDY PLANTS FROM SEED

The germination and subsequent treatment of all these half-hardy plants to be grown from seed is very similar and there is no need to distinguish between the annuals and the perennials. All will germinate rapidly in a temperature of 16° to 18°C. (60° to 65°F.) and some of the hardier kinds, such as the asters, stocks, zinnias and annual scabious, will be satisfied with 13°C. (55°F.). These can, in fact, be sown outdoors in late April or early May when the average temperature should be in that region.

It helps a lot if a propagating frame, however small, or even a box covered with glass, is available in the greenhouse, for in this it will be much easier to maintain a steady temperature without much expense. If electricity is laid on an electric air-warming cable can be placed in the frame or box, or you can buy a small propagator complete with electric heater. This does not necessarily mean that no heating will be required in the house itself, but the heating can almost certainly be at a lower level, and the difference in cost between maintaining a greenhouse at 7°C. (45°F.) and maintaining it at 16°C. (60°F.) is quite astonishing.

Late February and early March is the time for most of the seed sowing, but the stocks and asters can wait until late March and the zinnias until early April.

Either John Innes seed compost or one of the few soilless composts based on peat, such as the University of California compost, can be used, both for seed germination and for growing on, but the soilless compost needs less watering than John Innes compost. The compost can be placed in ordinary wooden seed boxes, in plastic seed trays or in pots or pans, which may be either clay or plastic, but in all cases should be provided with ample drainage holes or slits. Waterlogged compost will kill seedlings as quickly as anything.

Level off the compost with a straight-edge and then press it lightly with a piece of smooth flat wood to get a firm, level surface. Scatter the seed thinly over this and then sift a little of the compost over the seed (but very small seeds, such as those of the begonia, need no covering). Finally, place a sheet of glass and one of paper over each box or pan.

Germination may take from a week to three weeks according to variety and temperature available. The paper coverings should be removed as soon as the seedlings are seen, and the glass a day or so later. A week or ten days later the seedlings will probably be ready for pricking off, i.e. they must be very carefully transplanted so that each seedling is properly spaced and has room to grow into a sturdy little plant. The same kind of compost as that used for germination will be suitable, and as a rule it is most convenient to prick off into seed boxes, spacing the seedlings about 1½ in. apart each way. At this spacing an ordinary wooden seed box measuring 14 by 8½ in. will hold 54 seedlings. If you are dealing with much smaller numbers you can prick off into pots or pans, but they do not pack quite so well on the greenhouse staging or in the frame.

PRICKING-OFF

It is worth taking a good deal of trouble to prick-off the seedlings with as little injury to their roots as possible. If the work is done really early this will not be difficult, and they can be lifted a few at a time from the seed boxes or pans with a wooden tally and then, after being carefully singled out, can be planted in holes made with a pointed stick known as a dibber. But if for some reason the seedlings have grown so much that they cannot be lifted easily in this way, it is better to tip out the whole contents of the seed box or pot and then carefully disentangle the roots, than to risk breaking a lot of them.

Make the soil firm around the roots with fingers or dibber and, when a box or pan has been filled with seedlings, water it thoroughly using a watering can fitted with a fine rose. This will keep the seedlings fresh while they are getting established, and will settle the soil closely around their roots.

The pricked-off seedlings should then be placed on the greenhouse staging. It may be necessary to shade them for a few days, especially if the weather is bright; certainly they should not be allowed to flag badly at this stage. They must be watered before the soil becomes dry, but too much water at first may check rather than assist growth.

PLANTING OUT

The planting out of these half-hardy plants can seldom be done with safety before late May because of the danger of sharp night frost before that date. In the North of England and parts of Scotland it may even be necessary to delay until the first or second week in June. Only in very mild places, particularly near the south and west coasts, can early or mid-May planting be contemplated.

In any case the seedlings should not go direct from warm greenhouse to cold outdoors. They must have a fortnight or so of acclimatisation or hardening off. This is most conveniently given in a frame, because the protecting light can be left on if frost threatens or be removed altogether if the weather is mild.

A great many half-hardy plants are kept in the boxes in which they were pricked out right up to the time of planting out. This is all right as long as they do not get starved or overcrowded, but if they show any signs of either they should be potted individually. Quite small pots will do, 2½ in. or 3 in. in diameter, but this time a rather richer compost must be used, either the John Innes potting compost or one of the soilless composts with fertiliser added as recommended by the makers.

SOWING OUT OF DOORS

The outdoor sowings may include three groups of plants. First there are hardy annuals. They can be sown where they are to flower and later the seedlings can be thinned out so that they are not over-crowded. Usually the seedlings transplant quite well, so the thinnings, if lifted carefully with plenty of roots, can be used to fill up gaps. March and April are good months for sowing hardy annuals, but even May is not too late, and from such sowings plants will be obtained that will flower in August and September.

It is also possible to sow some of the hardiest of hardy annuals, plants such as larkspur, calendula, eschscholzia, nigella, clarkia, godetia and candytuft, in late or early September. The seedlings will be sturdy enough to overwinter without protection and they will be ready to flower the following summer well ahead of the spring-sown annuals. But there is risk of considerable loss of seedlings if the soil is badly drained or the winter is a very cold one.

In addition to the genuine hardy annuals, there are some half-hardy annuals that can be sown outdoors in late April or May, notably asters and zinnias as I have already stated. The plants will flower later than those raised under glass but that can be very useful. One does not want all the colour from annuals to come in June, July and early August with nothing to follow.

PLANTS FOR WINTER, SPRING AND EARLY SUMMER

All these annuals and half-hardy bedding plants are summer flowering. For winter

Seedlings of half-hardy perennials and half-hardy annuals which have been raised in a warm greenhouse are gradually hardened off in a frame for a fortnight or so before being planted out

and spring one must turn to two other groups, the hardy biennials and early-flowering perennials that grow quickly from seed. These include wallflowers *(Cheiranthus cheiri),* the Siberian wallflower *(C. allionii),* polyanthus, double daisies, pansies, forget-me-nots and Canterbury bells.

All can be raised from seed, the seedlings being planted out in rows in a bed reserved for this purpose, and grown on until the summer-flowering plants have been cleared away when these, the spring bedding plants, can be put in their place. But there generalisations must cease and each plant must receive its own appropriate treatment.

Polyanthus needs to be sown earliest, if possible in February or March, in a greenhouse or frame with a temperature of around 13°C. (55°F.). Subsequently, the resulting seedlings are pricked off into boxes and later planted out, much as if they were half-hardy annuals, except that they are planted in a nursery bed, not in a display bed. They may begin to produce a few flower buds in the autumn, but these should be picked off so that the plants build up good crowns to flower really freely the following spring.

Next in order of sowing time come the wallflower and Siberian Wallflower, double daisies (bellis) and Canterbury bells, all to be sown in May and June.

Forget-me-nots grow so rapidly that there is no need to sow them before the latter half of June. Pansies I sow in late June or July. There is a specially useful type of pansy known as Winter-flowering, which starts to flower very early. I use it a lot in my spring displays.

All these plants get the same subsequent treatment and go into their flowering beds in the autumn as soon as these have been cleared of summer occupants; but with wallflowers it does pay to get all planting finished in September, as then the plants are far less likely to suffer in winter.

DISPLAY PLANTS FROM CUTTINGS

Some of the finest summer-flowering display plants are perennials which can be conveniently and cheaply raised from cuttings. Into this category come geraniums (technically pelargoniums), marguerites, the grey-leaved *Centaurea gymnocarpa* and *Cineraria maritima*, penstemons, bedding calceolarias, fuchsias, chrysanthemums and dahlias. I say more about the last two in Chapters Fifteen and Sixteen respectively, and I shall confine myself to the others here.

Cuttings are most conveniently taken in

Left : Preparing penstemon cuttings from firm, non-flowering stems removed from the plants in late summer. Right : The cuttings being inserted in sandy soil in a frame after the base of each cutting has been dipped in rooting powder

August and September, for then the plants will be growing freely in the summer beds and a few shoots can be cut from each without being missed. Firm, non-flowering shoots are best, but if there are not enough of these any young growths can be used after removal of the flowers.

The cuttings should be 3 or 4 in. long. Each is cut straight through at the bottom, just below a joint, i.e. where a leaf or leaves are attached to the stem. The bottom leaves are removed, the base of the cutting is dipped in hormone rooting powder, which can be bought from any dealer in garden sundries, and then the cuttings are inserted in holes about 1 in. deep made with a dibber in sandy soil. A good compost for cuttings consists of equal parts (by vol.) soil, coarse sand and peat, but quite a lot will root in ordinary garden soil with a little sand and peat raked in. Every August I root some geranium cuttings outdoors without any protection at all, but by September it is better to put the cuttings in pots or boxes so that they can be brought into a frost-proof greenhouse or frame directly frost threatens.

Penstemons and calceolarias are nearly hardy and can be overwintered in a frame without any artificial heat. Violas can be grown in the same way, but nowadays there are such excellent seed strains available that not many gardeners bother with cuttings.

Geranium and fuchsia cuttings root very quickly and indicate when they have done so by starting to grow again. This is the signal to tap them out of their pots (or lift them if they were rooted outdoors) and pot them individually. Quite small pots will do, $2\frac{1}{2}$ in. for fuchsias, 3 in. or $3\frac{1}{2}$ in. for the geraniums. Either John Innes potting compost or soilless compost plus fertiliser will do for all of them, and the best place for them is on the staging in a light greenhouse with a minimum temperature of 7°C. (45°F.).

Cuttings also root readily in March and April so if you are short of plants you can insert some more then. This is what I always do with two of my favourite carpeting plants, the verbenas Loveliness and Lawrence Johnston. I root some cuttings in August and September, overwinter the resulting plants in the greenhouse, and then take more cuttings from them in early spring.

The only difference in the treatment of spring cuttings is that they need a little warmth (a temperature of 16 to 18°C. (60 to 65°F.) is ideal) and root more readily in a propagating frame or a box covered with a pane of glass—anything, in fact, that will reduce air circulation and keep the air around them moist.

CHAPTER THREE

More About Bedding Plants

I HAVE already said a good deal about the cultivation of bedding plants, but before passing on to describe some of the ways in which they may be used in the garden, I want to mention the training of plants, which can make so much difference to their effectiveness. Amateur gardeners, I think, are too ready to accept plants as they are. Those gardeners, like myself, who are responsible for public parks know that some plants, though beautiful in their natural habit, can be made to serve other useful purposes by being trained.

FORMS OF TRAINING

Standards

I am especially fond of fuchsias and, though I grow a great many as bushes with no more regulation of their natural habit than to make it even bushier by occasionally pinching out the tips of shoots, I also grow a lot of standard fuchsias.

These are quite easy to form and if you have a greenhouse you can easily do it for yourself. Start with cuttings in August. When these are rooted and potted, place a cane to each plant and keep the main growth tied to this so that it is absolutely straight and erect.

All side growths are removed until the main stem is about 5 ft. high, and then the top of the plant is pinched out to make it branch. What you want are six or eight good branches near the top and any others can be removed. When these side growths are themselves 6 or 8 in. long, they are pinched again to make even more branches, and so produce a really good 'head' of growth at the top of the main stem.

If the fuchsias are kept in a greenhouse with a temperature of around 13°C. (55°F.) they will go on growing all the winter and so, by the time the summer bedding is to be put out in late May or early June, they will be good, big plants, very useful for dotting here and there among the shorter plants to give height and variety to the beds. But they do need a lot of water during the summer, and to keep them flowering well into the autumn they should be given feeds of liquid manure.

Once formed these standards can be kept for years. They are lifted and potted in the autumn and brought under cover, but no attempt is made to keep them growing, as it was the first year when they were formed. Instead, they are permitted to take a rest until late February, when they are pruned, all side growths being shortened to 2 or 3 in. They are then knocked out of their pots, most of the soil is teased from their roots with a pointed stick, and then they

This planting of geraniums, alyssum, lobelia, gladioli and standard fuchsias provides bold colouring over a lengthy period. These plants are well suited to the built-up—but nevertheless open—surroundings of many new towns and suburbs

are repotted, watered and kept in a cool greenhouse to start them into growth.

Geraniums, as well as heliotrope (Cherry Pie), can be trained as standards in the same way and can be very decorative.

Pegging Down

There are other plants, naturally low growing, which can be made even more useful by a little training and pegging down. This can be done with annual phlox, verbena and ivy-leaved geraniums. If some fairly stout galvanised wire is cut into 6 in. lengths, and these are bent like hairpins, they can be put over the trailing shoots and pushed into the soil to hold them where they are required to cover the soil with a continuous carpet of growth and flowers.

CHOICE OF BEDDING PLANTS

Everyone will want to work out original schemes with bedding plants, but I intend now to describe some that I find pleasing for summer display.

I like to make a groundwork of light mauve-purple heliotrope (I use the variety W. H. Lowther) and edge it with silver- and green-leaved geraniums, for which I use the variety Little Dandy. Then I put in one or two standard plants of a free-flowering deep red fuchsia named Lord Leverhulme, to grow above the heliotrope, and a few plants of *Calocephalus brownii* (syn. *Leucophyta brownii*) which has thin, silver stems and can be trained to form erect columns of growth.

I find the scarlet salvia the hardest of all colours to place because it is so brilliant and there is so little green with it. So to break up this mass of dazzling colour I use *Fuchsia* Mrs Marshall grown as a standard, some big plants of silver-leaved *Centaurea gymnocarpa,* orange-flowered cannas with green leaves and an edging of white alyssum or Little Dandy geranium.

I also use *Fuchsia* Mrs Marshall, but bushy plants, not standards, with the red *Begonia* Flamboyant and bring in *Chrysanthemum ptarmicaeflorum* for silver and

[27]

Left : Lifting winter-flowering pansies in autumn for planting in display beds. Separate colours look more effective than mixtures in small beds. Right : Pegging down verbena stems with pieces of bent wire

Golden Feather, *Chrysanthemum parthenium aureum* (syn. *Matricaria eximia aurea*) for yellowish-green, with *Iresine aurea* for a stronger yellow foliage colour.

The peach-coloured *Begonia* Helen Harmes is one of my favourites. With this I mix the purple *Fuchsia* Brutus, dark red *Iresine lindeni* and silver chrysanthemum, and surround it all with the dark blue *Lobelia* Crystal Palace.

Another splendid begonia is Thousand Wonders, with pale pink flowers. With this I plant the bright red and bronze *Iresine herbstii brillantissima*, silver pyrethrum and *Lobelia* Cambridge Blue, and I put in a few plants of *Fuchsia* Thalia, which has red flowers and crimson leaves.

Some of the red varieties of *Begonia semperflorens* have dark bronze leaves, and a silver-leaved plant such as *Cineraria maritima* (syn. *Senecio cineraria*) or silver chrysanthemum livens these up most attractively. For further foliage colour I may add yellow *Iresine aurea*.

I like to make beds of salmon-pink geraniums with an edging of *Lobelia* Cambridge Blue and a few silver-leaved dot plants. With scarlet geraniums I bring

in both silver and golden variegated plants, including the tall *Abutilon striatum thompsonii* which makes a standard above the geraniums. Here again I can use *Fuchsia* Mrs Marshall, as a standard, and I edge it all with white alyssum or Little Dandy geranium.

For spring display I rely mainly on polyanthus, wallflowers and winter-flowering pansies.

The wallflowers I either grow in random mixture, all the colours together, or else in quite separate beds of colour. I have never been very happy with two or three varieties mixed in blocks of colour in a bed.

I have tried polyanthus in separate colours, but from seed there is usually some variation and I have come to the conclusion that they look better mixed.

I also like the winter-flowering pansies mixed, especially in large beds or borders, but in smaller beds I do use separate colours, particularly Celestial Queen which is pale blue; Helios, golden-yellow; March Beauty, deep purple; North Pole, white; and Wine Red which is really magenta and looks very well on its own with a surround of rich green grass.

[28]

CHAPTER FOUR

A Selection of Annuals

FOR convenience annuals are divided into two categories, hardy and half-hardy, but it must be understood that the division is an arbitrary one. In fact, no hard and fast line can be drawn, for what is hardy in Penzance might be half-hardy in Aberdeen. Moreover, though it is broadly true that hardy annuals are sown outdoors where they are to flower, whereas half-hardy annuals are sown under glass, to be planted out when danger of frost is past, there are exceptions on both sides. Sweet alyssum is fully hardy, yet millions of plants are raised commercially in greenhouses each spring and sold to the public in boxes. Asters and zinnias are genuine half-hardy annuals, yet both can be sown outdoors in late April and early May in many parts of the country, and some of the most successful growers invariably treat zinnias in this way, contending that the plants do better grown cool and without any break.

Nearly all annuals like sun and most have a very wide tolerance of soils, though they do best in those of rather open texture in which good crumbly seed beds can be prepared. They are easy to grow, too, and as they will be in full flower within a very short time, they are ideal plants with which to furnish the new garden while more permanent plans are being prepared. Prac-tically all you need to do to annuals, once they have been planted and thinned out, is to keep them free from the competition of weeds and to pick off the faded flowers before seeds begin to form. Weeds will starve the plants and make the beds untidy. Plants that are allowed to form seeds will soon stop flowering.

Here are a few good kinds to grow for colour:

HARDY ANNUALS

Alyssum. One of the most popular of all edging plants and also one of the easiest to grow. On a light soil, once you have sown or planted alyssum, you will probably never need to sow it again as self-sown seedlings will come up year after year. Choose a good compact variety such as Little Dorrit with pure white, fragrant flowers, and if you want a change in colour grow Violet Queen or Rosie O'Day with violet and rose flowers respectively.

Calendula. Probably the easiest to grow of all annuals and even more likely than alyssum to become a permanent occupant of the garden. Unfortunately self-sown seedlings usually deteriorate in quality rapidly, and it is wise to pull them out and renew each year from purchased seed.

Good varieties are Radio, deep orange; Golden King, yellow; and Geisha Girl, orange with incurving petals rather like a chrysanthemum. All grow 2 ft. high.

Candytuft (see Iberis)

Centaurea cyanus (Cornflower). The taller cornflowers, which may reach a height of 3 ft., are excellent for cutting but not very serviceable in the border, for which purpose the dwarf kinds, such as Jubilee Gem, 1 ft. high with cornflower-blue flowers; Lilac Lady, similar in height but with lilac flowers; and Polka Dot in a mixed range of colours are most suitable.

Chrysanthemum. The annual chrysanthemums are not to be confused with the perennial kinds grown in border and greenhouse. There are three distinct types, those derived from the Tricolor Chrysanthemum (*C. carinatum*), most of which have a band of deep colour dividing the central yellow disc from the lighter colour outside, those from the Garland Chrysanthemum (*C. coronarium*), which have either single or double flowers in self colours, and those from the Corn Marigold (*C. segetum*), many of which have a dark central disc. Most are between 1½ and 2 ft. high. There are many varieties in mixture. Golden Glory is a good single variety of the Garland type and Golden Gem is a good double variety. Eastern Star with yellow petals and a dark disc; Evening Star, golden-yellow throughout; and Southern Star (also known as Eldorado), canary yellow and black, are fine varieties of the Corn Marigold.

Clarkia. A good many hardy annuals produce their flowers in flat heads. Clarkias, by contrast, carry their flowers in narrow spikes which make a useful contrast in form. They also have a fine range of colour from white through pale pink and salmon-

This colourful combination of alyssum, tagetes (marigolds) and other annuals distracts the eye from the hard lines of the path. This is a form of display for which annuals of many kinds are admirably suited

rose, to carmine and crimson. Good varieties are Salmon Bouquet, Salmon Pink, Firebrand, Brilliant and White Queen.

Convolvulus. The annual varieties of convolvulus bring some of the richest shades of blue and purple into the garden. They are trailing plants 8 to 12 in. in height and sun lovers. Typical varieties are Royal Ensign, with wedgwood-blue flowers, and Royal Marine, a deep royal blue in colour.

Coreopsis. The annual varieties of coreopsis are usually listed in catalogues under their obsolete botanical name *Calliopsis*. They are daisy flowers usually in shades of yellow with crimson or maroon. Separate colours can be purchased such as Garnet, Crimson King and Tiger Star, but this is another flower I like to see in mixture. The plants grow 2 to 2½ ft. high and will need the support of twiggy branches.

Cornflower (see Centaurea)

Delphinium, Annual (Larkspur). The Larkspurs are delphiniums but in gardens the name has been confined almost entirely to the annual varieties, delphinium being reserved for the perennials. The annuals are lovely flowers with long slender spikes of bloom, and a wonderful colour range from white through palest lavender and pink to violet and crimson. The very finest flowers are obtained by sowing in early autumn, but good results can also be had from a spring sowing. Good varieties are Los Angeles, rose; Rosy Scarlet and Lilac Spire, well described by their names; Blue Spire, deep blue, and Carmine King, rosy-scarlet. All grow 3 to 4 ft. high.

Eschscholzia. Another annual inclined to take charge of the garden if you allow it to and one that, like calendula, will then decline in quality very rapidly. Modern strains have a wonderful colour range from white and pale yellow to orange and crimson, amber, pink and rose. Good mixtures of both singles and doubles can be obtained or separate colours can be purchased such as Mandarin, deep orange; Moonlight, light yellow; Dazzler, scarlet; and Toreador, crimson and bronze.

Giant-flowered Candytuft (see Iberis)

Godetia. There are two distinct types of godetia, the Azalea-flowered or Whitneyi varieties which make compact, freely branched plants 12 to 18 in. high, and the Grandiflora or Schamini varieties which carry their flowers in spikes 2 ft. or more in height. I think for display in the garden the Azalea-flowered varieties are the more desirable. First-class mixtures can be obtained giving a range of colour from white

to crimson, but this is an annual that looks well in blocks of a colour, good varieties being Sybil Sherwood, salmon-pink; Kelvedon Glory, salmon-rose; Lavender Queen, clear lavender; and Vivid, cherry-red.

Iberis (Candytuft). The flowers are produced in flattish heads in the common Candytuft and in fat spikes in the Giant-flowered or Rocket Candytuft. The Rocket Candytuft is white but the Common Candytuft has a good range of colour from white to crimson. Heights 10 to 18 in.

Larkspur (see Delphinium)

Lathyrus odoratus (Sweet Pea). The ordinary sweet peas can be used as a background to the annual border, grown naturally, without stopping or removing side shoots on pea sticks. Alternatively, groups of them can be used to form columns of colour at the back of the border. However, the possibilities with sweet peas have now been greatly increased by the introduction of really good dwarf varieties, such as Burpee's Early Dwarf Bijou, which only grows 12 in. high and has an excellent colour range.

Lavatera. This is one of the larger annuals making big bushy plants 2 or 3 ft. in height and as much through, but with stems so sturdy that they are well able to support themselves. The finest variety is Loveliness with large mallow-like flowers of a gleaming rose colour.

Love-in-a-Mist (see Nigella)

Mignonette (see Reseda)

Nasturtium (see Tropaeolum)

Nigella. This is the Love-in-a-Mist, so called because the flowers, typically blue and a little like cornflowers, are carried in a haze of the fine fern-like leaves. However, the colour range of nigella has been increased by the introduction of Monarch Persian Rose, a pink-flowered variety, and Monarch Persian Jewels, a mixture which includes pink, rose, purple and mauve. All grow $1\frac{1}{2}$ to 2 ft. high.

Phacelia. Another of the outstanding blue annuals. *P. campanularia* is a carpeter only a few inches in height with bell-shaped flowers which are a rich gentian blue. Give it a sunny place.

Reseda odorata (Mignonette). This is not a showy flower but it is deliciously fragrant and has the merit of associating well with any of the bright colours to be found in the annual border and helping to break them up. Mignonette does best in a soil that contains some lime. There are several named varieties but perhaps they do not differ very greatly one from another. Red Monarch and Crimson Giant have more colour in their green and red flowers than most and are also remarkable for their size.

Rocket Candytuft (see Iberis)

Sweet Pea (see Lathyrus)

Tropaeolum (Nasturtium). The old-fashioned nasturtiums that ramble all over the place are not much use in the modern garden except to form a quick screen over unsightly objects. For the annual border the various dwarf or Tom Thumb nasturtiums are the ones to grow. Many have double or semi-double flowers. Golden Gleam, with bright yellow flowers, is one of the most popular and Fiery Festival, with scarlet flowers, is also good. The mixture called Jewel Mixed, introduced several years ago, has fewer leaves than most and carries its flowers, in many different colours, well above the leaves.

HALF-HARDY ANNUALS

Ageratum. First-rate plants to edge a border or provide the groundwork beneath taller flowers. They give an altogether softer effect than lobelia. Some varieties, such as Blue Bedder, with lavender-blue flowers, grow only 4 in. high, but others, such as Blue Mink with larger

Left : The dimorphotheca hybrids in shades of buff, apricot, salmon and orange are sun-loving half-hardy annuals of unusual charm. Right : Petunia Pink Satin, *rose-pink, is one of the many fine varieties of this very popular summer bedding flower, available in a wonderful colour range*

heads of fluffy, powder-blue flowers, grow from 6 to 8 in. high. There are also pink varieties such as Fairy Pink, and good mixtures of colours.

Aster. The annual asters are often listed in catalogues under their obsolete botanical name *Callistephus*. There are both single- and double-flowered types and in the doubles a considerable range of flower styles, from the compact round blooms of the Powderpuff and Ball varieties to the large shaggy flowers of the Ostrich Plume asters. Heights, too, vary from 1 to 2½ ft. and in each group there is a good range of colour, from white, light lavender and soft pink to violet and crimson.

Dimorphotheca. This delightful South African annual brings a whole range of unusual colours to the garden. A good mixture of *D. aurantiaca* will cover buff, apricot, salmon and orange. Alternatively, separate colours can be purchased.

Livingstone Daisy (see Mesembryanthemum)

Lobelia. Strictly speaking a half-hardy perennial, but lobelia is almost invariably grown as a half-hardy annual and so I include it here. It is, with alyssum and ageratum, the most popular of all edging and groundwork plants, but choose a lobelia that really is compact in habit. Reliable varieties are Crystal Palace Improved, very deep blue, and Cambridge Blue, light blue. A recently introduced strain called String of Pearls gives a mixture of colours including white, pink, blue and violet.

Marigold (see Tagetes)

Mesembryanthemum. Most mesembryanthemums are perennials but the Livingstone Daisy, *M. criniflorum*, is a splendidly colourful half-hardy annual with daisy-like flowers in a wide range of colours of exceptional brilliance. It sprawls flat on the ground and makes an admirable carpet or edging, but its flowers only open in sunshine, so face it south if possible.

Nemesia. The lovely varieties of *N. strumosa* cover a cheerful range of colours. They look wonderful in mixture or in blocks of one colour. Choose good compact varieties such as Aurora, crimson and white, Blue Gem, Orange King and Fire King, scarlet.

Nicotiana (Tobacco Plant). The fragrant tobaccos, varieties of *N. affinis,* are comparatively tall plants, 2 to 3 ft. high, but they do not require staking. Unlike many annuals, they will grow well in partly shaded places. Some varieties only open their flowers towards evening, but Daylight keeps its white flowers open all day and so does Dwarf White Bedder, a shorter variety. The varieties of *N. sanderae,* such as Crimson Bedder, Crimson King and Knapton Scarlet, have flowers in shades of rose and red.

Petunia. These are rapidly becoming the most popular of summer-bedding plants, and have been developed so rapidly by breeders that the number of varieties available is now bewildering. For garden display the varieties with medium-sized blooms are best, but the large petunias and double-flowered varieties look well in ornamental vases, window-boxes and so on. Wonderful colours are available, such as Satellite, rose and white; Polaris, violet and white; Sugar Plum, lavender, veined purple; Pink Satin, rose-pink; Red Satin, scarlet; Brass Band, light yellow; Blue Bedder, light blue; Comanche Improved, scarlet; and Blue Velvet, indigo blue. Cherry Tart, rose and white, and Honeybunch, pink, are good doubles.

Left : The golden-yellow and maroon Tagetes *(Marigold) Naughty Marietta is of medium height and is especially good for garden display. Right : Zinnias are very decorative flowers with a good colour range*

Phlox. Individually the flowers of the annual phlox are not unlike those of the perennial phlox, but the habit of the plants is quite different as the stems are thin and they trail along the ground producing a jewelled mosaic of brilliantly coloured flowers. The colour range is from white to crimson and violet with some light yellows and buffs but no strong yellows.

Rudbeckia. This was an annual that did not attract much attention until the introduction of the large-flowered tetraploid varieties now sold as Gloriosa Daisies. These make big plants 3 to 4 ft. high with large, very showy, daisy-like flowers in various shades of yellow, orange, mahogany-red and bronze. There are both single-flowered and double-flowered strains.

Tagetes (Marigold). In America the marigold is one of the most popular of all summer flowers and it is gaining in popularity in Britain thanks to the introduction of fine new varieties. The range of form is quite astonishing, from miniatures such

as the Petite strains, only 6 in. high, with flowers scaled to match, to the giant African varieties such as Golden Climax, light yellow; Primrose Climax, primrose-yellow; Yellow Climax, bright yellow; and Toreador, orange. For garden display some of the medium-height marigolds take a lot of beating, and blend in better than the big mop heads. Good varieties are Naughty Marietta and Legion of Honour, both golden-yellow blotched with maroon and both 9 in. high. For edging there is the 6 in. *Tagetes signata pumila* with single orange flowers.

Tobacco Plant (see Nicotiana)

Zinnia. The familiar zinnia grows 2 to $2\frac{1}{2}$ ft. high and has big ball-shaped flowers with flat petals, but a strain has been developed with quilled petals like chrysanthemums, and there is also a miniature strain, known as Thumbelina, 6 in. high, with neat little double flowers, in the full range of zinnia colours—yellow, orange, scarlet, magenta and rose.

[34]

The colour of massed rhododendrons—and even more of massed azaleas—can be extremely effective but also rather overwhelming unless one disciplines oneself to plant with restraint. In this planting there is a preponderance of blue, yellow and white with just a small amount of red

A water-lily pool, even of modest size, provides an opportunity to grow an exciting collection of moisture-loving plants in its environs. Here, are Primula bulleyana, P. japonica, helianthemums, violas, golden yew and other colourful plants

Ground cover plants providing a medley of autumnal colours with their own distinctive charm. The plants in the pathside planting include variegated sage (top right) the large-leaved Bergenia cordifolia, flower spikes of Polygonum affine Lowndes Variety and Geranium macrorrhizum (on the right)

In contrast to the display on the left this cool—and also very pleasing—scene holds out no threat of failure. The attractive, soft colours in this herbaceous border would be in harmony with almost any other garden feature. The stone path forms a natural bridge between the flowers and the lawn. If the salvias

The bed of hot-coloured salvias has its perfect foil in the multi-toned greens which flow away into the distance. The accent is on contrast, which has been achieved. With plants as richly coloured as these salvias, though, the home gardener is playing with fire—the dividing line between success

Concerning Hardy Plants

HARDY plants or herbaceous perennials, whichever you prefer to call them, are the backbone of a great many gardens. Unlike annuals and bedding plants, they will go on for years without renewal or disturbance, though this is not the best way to grow many of them. Some, such as peonies, Japanese anemones and hellebores, positively dislike being moved but they are in a minority. Most hardy plants benefit from being lifted and divided every third or fourth year. Michaelmas daisies produce their finest flowers when lifted and divided annually.

Few hardy plants are fussy about soil. Some, such as pyrethrums, gaillardias and anthemis, dislike heavy, badly drained soil and the leaves of lupins may be yellow where there is much chalk or lime. But in general if the soil is well broken up with spade or fork and given a scattering of a good all-purpose fertiliser, hardy plants will grow and flower freely.

The taller kinds may need quite a lot of staking but hardy plants up to about 3 ft. tall will either stand up on their own, or find all the support they require from a few short hazel stems or other twiggy branches pushed in around them in spring, so that the stems grow through the sticks and conceal them.

SOME EASY KINDS

Here are some good easy kinds with which to begin:

Achillea (Yarrow). I have already stressed the importance of white flowers to break up the strong colours without dulling them (see p. 9). For this purpose *Achillea* The Pearl is in the first rank as its small double white flowers are freely produced from June to August on plants 2 to 3 ft. high that need little or no staking. *A.* Coronation Gold has flat heads of yellow flowers over grey ferny leaves from June to September. *A. taygetea* and Moonshine repeat this in sulphur yellow, but do not flower for so long.

Aconitum (Monkshood). The Monkshoods are fine plants though not widely grown perhaps because they are poisonous —but for that matter so are Christmas Roses and Lilies-of-the-valley. However, there are not so many blue spike-flowered perennials that we can afford to neglect any as good as these. One of the best, because it needs little or no staking, is Bressingham Spire, 3 ft. high, violet-blue and flowering in July and August.

Alkanet (see Anchusa)

Anchusa (Alkanet). For early blue in the

middle and back of the border *A. italica* is the plant in one or other of its numerous varieties, such as Loddon Royalist, 3 ft. gentian blue; Morning Glory, 5 ft. dark blue; and Opal, 4 ft. light blue. All bloom in late May or June. They like sunshine and well-drained soil.

Anemone (Windflower). The Japanese anemones (varieties of *A. hybrida,* quite often listed incorrectly as *A. japonica*) are valuable for their late-flowering in August and September when their saucer-shaped flowers in white, pink or rose make a pleasant change from the prevailing Michaelmas daisies. Heights vary from 2 ft. to 4 ft. Good varieties are Whirlwind, white; Queen Charlotte, pale pink; and Profusion, deep pink.

Artemisia. Most of the artemisias are shrubs, but *A. lactiflora* is a fine herbaceous plant, 5 ft. tall with elegant plumy sprays of small white flowers in August and September. It is another of those whites so useful for breaking up the strong colours.

Aster (Michaelmas Daisies). All the host of Michaelmas daisies must be considered here, starting in August with the bushy *amellus* varieties, of which the single blue King George, 2 ft., is still the most popular, and finishing up with the bewilderingly numerous varieties of *novi-belgii.* Most of these are 3 or 4 ft. high and need some staking and fairly frequent division, too, if they are not to get untidy. But there are also dwarf varieties such as the light blue Audrey, 15 in.; the rich blue Lady in Blue, 10 in.; and the cerise Jenny, 12 in.

Astilbe. These are the plants often called spiraea, with plume-like sprays of flowers in July and August. They dislike hot, dry places. Heights are mostly around 2½ to 3 ft., except for the varieties of *A. simplicifolia* which are 12 in. or less. Good varieties

of normal height are Fanal, garnet red; Red Sentinel, turkey red; Rheinland, clear pink; Deutschland and White Queen, white.

Campanula. Many of the campanulas are rock garden plants but there are big herbaceous kinds, too, one of the tallest being *C. lactiflora,* 5 ft., with loose clusters of light blue cup-shaped flowers in July and August. Loddon Anna is a mauve-pink counterpart and Pouffe a remarkable cushion-like variety only a foot high. In the intermediate height range, 2 to 3 ft., the varieties of *C. persicifolia,* blue or white and sometimes double-flowered, are useful. *C. glomerata dahurica* is a splendid violet-purple species with flowers in June-July tightly clustered on 12 in. stems. The 9 in. tall, July-August flowering *C. carpatica* which has blue or white flowers is a plant for the front of the border.

Catmint (see Nepeta)

Chrysanthemum. In addition to the annual chrysanthemums and the florist chrysanthemums there are hardy border varieties often called Shasta daisies or Moon Daisies. All are white, 2 to 3 ft. high and July-August flowering. Some such as Everest and Phyllis Smith are single flowered, some such as Esther Read and Wirral Supreme are double flowered, and some such as Wirral Pride are semi-double or anemone-centred: all make solid areas of white in the border.

Cone Flower (see Rudbeckia)

Day Lily (see Hemerocallis)

Delphinium. The delphiniums are the noblest and in some ways the most exciting of all herbaceous plants but they do need a little more management than most—careful staking, proper feeding, fairly frequent renewal from cuttings or seeds. There are first-rate seed strains such as the

Hardy herbaceous plants blend in well with many different garden features and settings. The plants (left) form a soft arc of colour from the back to the front of the border. The border on the right, on the other hand, reflects the variation in elevation of the trees in the background

Pacific Giants giving a wide range of colours, including white, lilac-pink, lavender, light blue, dark blue and purple. There are also a great many named varieties such as Blue Jade, light blue; Blackmore's Glorious, soft lilac and blue; Royalist, purple; and Silver Moss, silvery-lilac. Given good cultivation most of those will reach a height of 6 or 7 ft. Shorter varieties are now being raised and there are also the Belladonna varieties which branch freely and carry their flowers in sprays rather than in spikes. These are usually about 4 ft. high. Wendy, gentian blue, and Orion, cornflower blue, are typical.

Echinops (Globe Thistle). Known as the Globe Thistle because of the spiky globu-lar heads of blue or white flowers. Taplow Blue with dark blue flowers is one of the best. It grows 5 ft. tall. *E. ritro* is smaller, around 3 ft., and *E. sphaerocephalus* has off-white flowers. All bring a distinctive element to the border.

Erigeron. These look like Michaelmas daisies but are quite short and flower from June to August. Good varieties are Festivity, light blue, 2 ft.; Vanity, light pink, $2\frac{1}{2}$ ft.; and Foerster's Liebling, deep pink, $1\frac{1}{2}$ ft.

Eryngium (Sea Holly). These are the Sea Hollies, with teazle-like flower heads surrounded by ruffs of stiff bracts, which in some varieties are finely cut and attractively coloured. Like the Globe Thistles they are welcome because they are so different. Two good kinds are *E. tripar-titum* with many small metallic blue flowers and Violetta with fewer but much larger violet-blue flowers. Both bloom in July and August.

Gaillardia. Few perennials are capable of making so concentrated a display for two or three months, roughly from mid-summer to late August. The plants do, however, tend to wear themselves out and should be renewed fairly frequently from seed or root cuttings. Good varieties are Ipswich Beauty, deep yellow and red; Mandarin, orange-flame; Wirral Flame, reddish-bronze; and Mrs H. Longster, yellow with a small red zone. All grow about 2 ft. high and need bushy twigs for support. They like sunny places and well-drained soil.

Globe Thistle (see Echinops)

Golden Rod (see Solidago)

Gypsophila. These are useful for their lightness and elegance. The flowers are small but produced with the utmost free-dom in loose cloudy sprays. One of the best is Bristol Fairy with double white flowers. It grows 3 ft. tall. Flamingo repeats this in lilac-pink; Rosy Veil is also pink but only 12 in. tall. All flower from July to September.

Helenium. Useful because they give solid masses of yellow, bronze and crimson from mid to late summer. Good varieties are Butterpat, yellow, 3 ft., very late flowering; Wyndley, coppery-orange, 2 ft.; Moerheim Beauty, wallflower red, 3 ft. and Madame Canivet, light yellow with a dark centre, $2\frac{1}{2}$ ft.

Helianthus (Sunflower). These are the perennial sunflowers and many of them are too tall or too invasive for the ordinary garden. But two varieties of *H. multiflorus* which can be recommended, and need little or no support, are Loddon Gold, with large double golden-yellow flowers, and Capenoch Star with even bigger single flowers. Both flower in July and August and are 5 ft. tall.

Heliopsis. The effect is similar to that of the perennial sunflowers but there are some even richer shades of yellow. Light of Loddon is bright yellow, Golden Plume, golden-yellow, and Orange King, orange-yellow. All are about 4 ft. high and have such stiff stems that they need little support.

Hemerocallis (Day Lily). These are known as Day Lilies because the trumpet-shaped flowers resemble lilies and each lasts for one day only. This is not such a drawback as it sounds as buds are freely produced and flowers open in rapid suc-cession during July and August and some continue in September. The merits of the day lilies are that they are very easily grown, require no staking and bring a different style of flower into the border. There are a great many varieties but not a great colour range which is from pale yellow, through orange to deep mahogany-crimson. The soft colourings of many of them are attractive. Most are $2\frac{1}{2}$ to $3\frac{1}{2}$ ft. tall.

Kniphofia (Red Hot Poker and Torch Lily). These bring a highly distinctive flower shape to the border. The most familiar is *K. uvaria* with 4 ft. high red and yellow flower spikes in August and Sep-tember. Royal Standard, a little shorter, earlier and with rather more yellow and less red, is also popular. A quite recently intro-duced variety, Maid of Orleans, has cream flowers and is 3 ft. tall. Buttercup is deep yellow and may start to flower in June. It is 4 ft. tall. Despite their height none of these requires staking as the flower stems are thick and sturdy.

Lupin (see Lupinus)

Left : The sulphur yellow Achillea taygetea, *2 ft. or so tall and with greyish coloured foliage, is useful for its form and its colour. This yarrow flowers from June to August. Right : The softly coloured hemerocallis or Day Lilies are very easily grown and need no staking*

Lupinus (Lupin). The splendid Russell lupins, some in self colours, others combining two contrasted colours in the same flower, need no recommendation as they are among the most popular perennials. Unfortunately they tend to be short-lived and so should be fairly frequently renewed from seed or cuttings. Excellent seed strains are now available but these mostly give mixed colours.

Left : The coppery-orange Helenium Wyndley. *The showy heleniums provide solid masses of yellow, bronze and crimson colouring from mid to late summer. Right : The purple-flowered* Salvia superba *is a useful border plant and has a dwarf variety, East Friesland (below)* $1\frac{1}{2}$ *ft. tall*

Lythrum. The rather fierce magenta flower spikes need to be carefully placed in the garden but can be most effective. One of the best varieties is Robert, rosy-red; the Beacon is darker—a full carmine. Both are about 3 ft. tall and are self-supporting.

Michaelmas Daisies (see Aster)

Monkshood (see Aconitum)

Nepeta (Catmint). The catmint is a popular edging plant because its grey foliage looks attractive and it flowers non-stop from June to September. The flowers are lavender-blue and, in fact, the whole effect of this plant is comparable with that of lavender. The ordinary variety grows 18 in. high, but Six Hills Giant may reach 3 ft. in good soil.

Paeonia (Peony). The peonies are the most opulent border flowers in May and June and are quite indispensable. Unfortunately they resent disturbance and often sulk for a year or so after being transplanted. Buy young plants in September, give them good rich soil and keep them well watered the first summer. There are innumerable varieties, none more showy than the old Double Red and the single *P. lobata* (also known as *P. peregrina*). These, however, are not scented like the Chinese peonies such as Duchess de Nemours, creamy-white; Albert Crousse, bright pink; Sarah Bernhardt, rose; Solange, salmon; and Felix Crousse, red.

Papaver (Poppy). For the perennial border it is *P. orientale*, the Oriental Poppy, that matters. From this you will certainly get Oriental splendour in scarlet, pink and white for a few weeks in late May and June, but a good deal of untidyness later. Try to mask this by planting something that will grow up in front of the poppies

when they have faded. King George, scarlet; Mrs George Stobard, salmon-pink; and Perry's White are good varieties, all 3 ft. tall.

Peony (see Paeonia)

Phlox. The herbaceous phlox, like the peony in early summer, is quite indispensable in July, August and early September, both for solid masses of colour and fragrance. Good varieties are Brigadier, orange-red; Sir John Falstaff, salmon-pink; Mia Ruys, white; Eventide, lavender; Border Gem, violet; and William Kesselring, purple, but there are many more.

Physostegia. Some kinds are far too tall and straggly but not Vivid, a first rate front-row plant with little foot-high spikes of bright rose flowers which come in September and October when they are especially welcome.

Poppy (see Papaver)

Red Hot Poker (see Kniphofia)

Rudbeckia (Cone Flower). Some of the perennial kinds are very tall plants that may blow over if not supported, but *Rudbeckia* Goldsturm suffers from no such drawback as it grows only $2\frac{1}{2}$ ft. high and has stiff wiry stems. The large daisy flowers are very showy, deep yellow with a black central disc. They continue from July to September.

Salvia. The best hardy salvia for the border is *S. superba*. Its narrow purple spikes are produced in great abundance in July and August. The common form grows 3 ft. tall but Lubeca is shorter, about 2 ft., and East Friesland shorter still, only $1\frac{1}{2}$ ft.

Sea Holly (see Eryngium)

Sedum (Stonecrop). Most of the stonecrops are rock plants but *S. spectabile* is a splendidly showy border plant for the front row. Its great flat heads of pink flowers attract butterflies which add to their beauty. Brilliant is a deeper coloured variety. Both grow 18 in. high and flower in August and September.

Sidalcea. The slender pink spikes of the sidalcea help to break up the more solid masses of colour in the border. There are a lot of varieties and not much difference between some of them but Rev. Page Roberts is soft pink; Rose Queen, rose-pink, and Croftway Red as near red as sidalceas get. All are about 4 ft. high.

Solidago (Golden Rod). These were once regarded as common and rather weedy flowers but they have now been made valuable by the introduction of short, bushy varieties such as Lena, Leraft and Goldenmosa, all 2 or 3 ft. high with feathery masses of golden-yellow flowers in August and September.

Stonecrop (see Sedum)

Sunflower (see Helianthus)

Torch Lily (see Kniphofia)

Veronica. The slender blue or pink spikes of the herbaceous veronicas are another of the antidotes to too much solidity in the border. Avoid the very tall varieties and go for those of short to medium height such as *V. longifolia subsessilis,* rich purple; *V. incana* Wendy, with grey leaves and purple flowers; and *V. spicata* Barcarolle, pink. These all flower in late summer, but the light blue, 2 ft. tall *V. gentianoides,* flowers in May.

Windflower (see Anemone)

Yarrow (see Achillea)

Left : The herbaceous phlox, like the salmon-pink Sir John Falstaff below, are valuable plants for July to early September display. Right : The 2½-ft.-tall Rudbeckia Goldsturm is another excellent border plant, with deep yellow flowers marked with a black central disc

CHAPTER SIX

Shrubs for Colour

THE planning of a border of shrubs for colour does not present quite the same problems as one of herbaceous plants or annuals, except perhaps where rhododendrons and azaleas are to figure prominently, for their lavish colours, as already remarked (p. 12), can clash unless selected carefully. But with most shrubs the flowers are well balanced with green foliage which helps to avoid disharmony.

Shrubs can be had in flower in every month of the year and when planning a border they may be chosen to ensure the longest possible season of flower. Their form must also be taken into consideration, so that taller plants do not overcrowd those of dwarf habit, the lean and bony ones are balanced by those of more ample growth and foliage, and so on.

Special colour effects can also be created. It is possible to have gold and silver borders, making use of shrubs noted for their colourful foliage and stems as well as for their flowers. Heathers are becoming very popular and their colours combine well with the foliage of golden cupressus.

Evergreen shrubs are indispensable for the permanent colour effects they can create, and they also make splendid backgrounds to show up the flowers and foliage of other shrubs.

COLOUR MONTH BY MONTH
January
Cornus (Dogwood). The Dogwoods include species and varieties valuable for their colourful young stems in winter. Two excellent kinds are *Cornus alba atrosanguinea* with bright red stems and *C. stolonifera flaviramea* with yellow stems.

Dogwood (see Cornus)

Garrya. The male form of *G. elliptica* is commonly grown, as it is superior to the female for decoration because its slender grey-green catkins are much longer. This fine evergreen will reach a height of 8 to 10 ft. and be as much through.

Hamamelis mollis (Witch Hazel). The best Witch Hazel is *H. mollis*, the Chinese Witch Hazel, with curious yellow scented flowers that appear from December to February; the foliage is also colourful in autumn. Plants eventually grow 12 to 15 ft. tall, and as much in width, but this takes some years.

Salix (Willow). *Salix vitellina brizensis* is one of the finest willows for its red shoots, a lovely sight in winter. As the best colour is from the young bark, all are pruned hard each March to encourage plenty of new growth.

White flowers may not be every gardener's favourite but they have an indispensable role to play nevertheless. They will liven up the colours of other flowers, for instance, without causing offensive clashes of their own. Silver, too, is one of the most useful ingredients in the garden maker's palette for breaking down the dominance of strongly coloured plants near by. Green has a special value for the gardener for it is in harmony with all colours, and tones down the most aggressive

Summer bedding in a patio garden. Most of the colour is provided by
geraniums and fibrous-rooted begonias which blend so well together,
and with the water and stonework naturally associated with features of this
kind. Note the dwarf conifers which are used as 'point' plants to give
cohesion to the overall scene.

In this garden the floral display has been been allowed to spill out onto the road
verge with charming results. Note that the natural colourfulness of the
zinnias has been enhanced by their background of white fencing—another
illustration of the value of white. In this case, too, the white of the fence
finds its natural accompaniment in the walls of the house.

This formal planting scheme in the famous Keukenhof Gardens, Holland, relies entirely on bedding plants and the effect can be changed annually if so desired. Note how the planting of the orange Early Single tulip General de Wet sweeps round to the blue muscari and these find a mutually sympathetic bond in the green of the surrounding grass

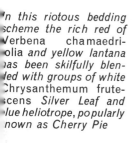

In this riotous bedding scheme the rich red of Verbena chamaedrifolia and yellow lantana has been skilfully blended with groups of white Chrysanthemum frutescens Silver Leaf and blue heliotrope, popularly known as Cherry Pie

This colourful border of annuals is an excellent example of the attractiveness of these easily grown flowers when well displayed. It must be understood, though, that the impact comes from their colours alone, not from their form. The plants shown here, all hardy annuals, include (from top to bottom) Lavatera Loveliness, *Chrysanthemum* Southern Star *and* Eschscholzia Autumn Glory. *Nearly all annuals like sun and most have a very wide tolerance of soils. For a quick display of colour in a new garden they are an ideal choice*

Willow (see Salix)

Witch Hazel (see Hamamelis)

February

Corylopsis. The most commonly grown species is *C. spicata*, a deciduous shrub with primrose-yellow flowers that appear before the leaves. The flowers can be spoilt by frost and a sheltered position away from early morning sun is desirable. The plants grow about 6 ft. tall and as much in width when mature.

Daphne. The species most commonly seen is *D. mezereum,* the Mezereon, with fragrant purple or white flowers before the leaves, from February to April. It grows rather narrowly upright to a height of 4 ft. and is excellent for small gardens. *D. burkwoodii,* growing only 3 ft. tall and as much through, has pale pink flowers in May.

Mezereon (see Daphne)

March

Chaenomeles (Japanese Quince). The Japanese Quinces, popularly known as Japonica or Cydonia, are valuable for their early spring flowers. They can be trained on walls or allowed to grow as bushes in a border. There are numerous varieties and hybrids of *C. speciosa* with pink, white or red flowers. Knap Hill Scarlet, orange-scarlet, makes a bush up to 6 ft. tall; Rowallane with bright red blooms grows to 4 ft.; and Moerloesii, apple-blossom pink, to 7 ft.

Forsythia. This is one of the easiest shrubs to grow and with very little attention will produce masses of yellow flowers each year, provided the birds do not pick out its buds in winter. One of the most popular kinds is *F. intermedia spectabilis* which will make a bush 10 ft. tall with rich deep yellow flowers. The variety Lynwood has even larger flowers. *F. suspensa atrocaulis* is notable for its purple stems which contrast with the pale yellow flowers.

Japanese Quince (see Chaenomeles)

April

Flowering Currant (see Ribes)

Pieris. The most striking kind is *P. forrestii* which not only has sprays of white flowers rather like Lily-of-the-Valley, but also young shoots which are bright red. It is an evergreen but must be grown in lime-free soil containing plenty of peat. Plants need a sheltered position and in good conditions will grow 7 ft. tall and as much across.

Ribes (Flowering Currant). The flowering currants, *R. sangineum* and its varieties, are easy-going shrubs that succeed in almost any soil and situation. It is best to plant specially selected forms such as Pulborough Scarlet or King Edward VII, both with deep crimson flowers. Most kinds grow 8 to 10 ft. tall and spread rapidly, but they can be hard pruned after flowering if it is necessary to keep them smaller.

May

Barberry (see Berberis)

Berberis (Barberry). There are deciduous and evergreen kinds of barberry notable for their flowers and/or berries. Two evergreens excellent for the shrub border are *B. stenophylla* and *B. darwinii*, both with deep yellow flowers. These are big shrubs, useful as background and growing to a height and spread of 8 to 10 ft.

Rhododendron. In addition to the well-known evergreen kinds, all the azaleas belong in this genus. The deciduous azaleas produce masses of flowers in a wealth of colours. Equally dazzling in their brightest forms, though containing some softer lavenders and pinks as well, are the dwarf evergreen azaleas such as Hinodegiri and Hinomayo. The hardy hybrid rhododendrons, including such well-known kinds as Pink Pearl and Britannia, scarlet, make large bushes with big trusses of flower in shades of red, blue, yellow and white. In addition there are some which have the additional attraction of handsome foliage. The leaves of *R. williamsianum* are round and only an inch or two across. Bushes of this form low mounds, not much more than 2 ft. in height and with delightful pink flowers.

All rhododendrons must have soil free from lime. They benefit from mulching each spring with moist peat or decayed leaves.

June

Cistus (Rock Rose). These shrubs are very free-flowering evergreens with blooms like some of the wild roses—hence the common name. They like a hot, sunny situation and well-drained soil. *C. purpureus* grows 4 to 5 ft. tall and about 6 ft. in width; the rose-pink flowers have a dark zone in the centre. Silver Pink is a good variety with pale pink flowers and *C. cyprius* has large white flowers. All are a little tender and may be killed in very severe winters such as that of 1962–63.

Jasminum. From late in the month until approximately late August the Summer Jasmine, *J. officinale,* provides a display with its fragrant white flowers, which are borne in profusion. This climber likes a sunny position.

Rock Rose (see Cistus)

Summer Jasmine (see Jasminum)

Weigela. Until recently called *Diervilla,* these are easily grown shrubs with masses of pink or red tubular flowers. There are numerous named varieties which include Bristol Ruby, light crimson; Styriaca, deep rose; and Newport Red, deep red. These grow about 6 ft. tall and a little more in width, but can be kept smaller by pruning after flowering, when the branches that have flowered can be cut out.

July

Buddleia. There are few shrubs that give such a good show for so little attention as the varieties of *B. davidii*. The flowers can be had in various shades of purple and lilac as well as white, and if the old stems are pruned hard in early March fine flower spikes are produced in the summer. Plants can be kept to a height of about 6 ft. by such annual pruning, and will have a similar spread. Another beautiful species with lavender flowers all along the stems is *B. alternifolia*. As the stems are pendulous it is best grown as a standard on a long main stem.

Senecio. *Senecio laxifolius* (syn. *S. greyi*) is a valuable shrub both for its grey evergreen foliage and its masses of yellow, daisy-like flowers in summer. It has a rather spreading habit and succeeds well in poor, well-drained soil in a sunny position. It is also good near the sea. Plants do not grow much more than 3 ft. in height but may be twice that in width.

August

Ceanothus. There are both evergreen and deciduous kinds but the latter tend to be hardier and more reliable, and they flower in late summer when the number of shrubs in bloom is far more restricted than in May-June, the season of the evergreen ceanothus. Gloire de Versailles, pale blue, and Henri Desfosse, deep violet, are good deciduous varieties. Their height and spread is 5 to 6 ft., if cut hard back each April.

Hibiscus. Valuable for their hollyhock-like flowers in late summer. There are numerous varieties of *H. syriacus*, such as Coeleste, blue; Woodbridge, red; and Souvenir de Charles Breton, lilac, double flowered. They will reach a height of about 8 ft. and nearly as much through but are slow growing.

Hydrangea. In addition to the familiar mop-headed hydrangeas, there are the less well-known Lacecaps with large coloured bracts surrounding a flattish disc of tiny flowers. There are numerous varieties of both types but the colour does depend on the soil. In lime-free soils the flowers tend towards blue and purple whereas on limy soils they tend towards pink and red. Alum applied to the soil can be used to change from red to blue but this is difficult if there is a lot of lime present. White varieties remain white whatever the soil. Two fine Lacecap varieties are Blue Wave, blue or lilac, and White Wave, white. Good mop-heads are Vicomtesse de Vibraye, light blue or pink; Westfalen, crimson or violet; Hamburg, deep pink or blue; and Madame E. Moulliere, white. The flower buds for the following year are formed at the tips of the shoots made in the previous year. In cold districts, where frost can damage the buds, flowering is not likely to be good unless protection is given.

September

Caryopteris. Particularly valuable for its late blue flowers and greyish foliage, *C. clandonensis* can grow 3 to 4 ft. tall and almost as much across, although plants can be kept shorter by pruning back the shoots each April. Two modern varieties with

Mop-headed hydrangeas with their soft rounded outline and profusion of flowers form a sympathetic bond with the facades of many houses

good dark blue flowers are Ferndown and Kew Blue.

Fuchsia. There are many varieties, with flowers as attractive as the greenhouse kinds, that can be grown in the open if the base of the plant is mounded with sand, peat or weathered ashes as protection in the winter. The stems may be cut back to ground level by frost but new growth should shoot from the base in the spring and flower in late summer. The fuchsia that is often seen near the sea is *F. magellanica riccartonii* which has small red and purple flowers. *F. m. gracilis versicolor* not only has carmine and purple flowers but attractive foliage variegated with silver and pink. Lena, pale pink and mauve; Margaret, carmine and parma violet; Corallina, scarlet and purple; and Mrs Popple, carmine and violet, are other varieties well worth growing.

Potentilla (Shrubby Cinquefoil). The varieties of *P. fruticosa* with bright yellow or white buttercup-like flowers are valuable for their long flowering season from June to October. Good varieties are *arbuscula* which makes a wide spreading low bush with yellow flowers; Katherine Dykes, 5 ft. high and through, yellow; and Mount Everest, 3 ft. high and through, white.

Shrubby Cinquefoil (see Potentilla)

October
Acer (Maple). Most of the maples are trees, but the varieties of *A. palmatum* are shrubby and valuable for their handsome foliage which colours magnificently in autumn. The leaves of the variety *purpureum* are deep purple throughout the summer and those of *dissectum atropurpureum* are not only purple throughout but also finely cut, like those of a fern. Both grow slowly and take years to reach a height of 6 to 8 ft.

Cotoneaster. The many kinds, both deciduous and evergreen, are of particular value for their berries, although the flowers are not uninteresting. *C. horizontalis* sends out its shoots horizontally, is deciduous and has masses of red berries. It looks particularly well against a wall or covering a rock. *C. conspicuus decorus* is an evergreen bush of rounded habit, 3 to 4 ft. high with scarlet berries. *C. franchetii* is a more open shrub with arching branches to 8 ft. and as much through, also with scarlet berries. *C. salicifolius* Herbstfleur, growing only 1 ft. tall, carpets ground quickly and is excellent on banks.

Fothergilla. The hazel-like leaves turn a lovely shade of yellow in the autumn and in April-May produce creamy-white flower spikes. *F. monticola* is one of the best kinds growing to a height and breadth of about 5 ft. No fothergilla grows well on lime or chalk soils.

November
Barberry (see Berberis)

Berberis (Barberry). It is the deciduous kinds that produce abundant crops of scarlet or coral berries in the autumn. *B. wilsonae* which makes a dense, spiny bush 4 to 5 ft. high is a fine example of this type and so are *B. aggregata* and *B. Cherry Ripe*.

Firethorn (see Pyracantha)

Pyracantha (Firethorn). The Firethorns are showy evergreen shrubs with masses of red or yellow berries in autumn and winter and abundant white flowers in May and June. They can be trained to walls—they do well with north aspects—or allowed to grow as bushes in the open. Most grow 10 ft. tall and as wide. *P. coccinea lalandii* with bright red berries is the type most commonly seen but the yellow-berried *P. rogersiana fructu-luteo* is very well worth growing.

Skimmia. An evergreen growing 3 to 4 ft. tall, with large bright red berries. The type to grow is *S. foremanii* as it has both male and female flowers on the same bush and bears regular crops of berries in the winter. It will grow well in shade.

December
Jasminum (Jasmine). The hardy *J. nudiflorum* (Winter Jasmine) is a fine climber for winter colour. It has yellow flowers and will grow even with a north aspect.

Viburnum. There are both deciduous and evergreen kinds, not all winter flowering. *V. tinus,* generally known as Laurustinus, starts to open its clusters of white flowers —pink in the bud stage—in late autumn and continues well into the spring. *V. fragrans* is deciduous with pretty pink and white scented flowers which appear from November to February. *V. bodnantense* has larger deeper pink flowers but a stiffer, slightly ungainly habit. All grow to a height of 10 ft.

Winter Jasmine (see Jasminum)

CHAPTER SEVEN

Trees for Colour

THE typical modern, fairly small garden may not give wide scope for the use of ornamental trees, but those that can be included in the scheme of things have an importance out of all proportion to their numbers. One should not forget when planning or re-modelling a garden the transformation in scale which can be brought about by planting only one or two trees in carefully chosen positions. Naturally one must choose trees of suitable dimensions, and consider which are likely to make the most valuable contribution to the general scheme of things—whether they have flowers of fine form and colouring, handsome leaves or bark, or just an elegance of habit which will give added point to other adjacent garden features.

COLOUR FOR ALL SEASONS

Acer (Maple). Many of the maples make large trees, too tall for small gardens, and the Japanese Maples (varieties of *A. palmatum*) have been described in the previous chapter on shrubs (see p. 52), but intermediate between these there are species and varieties supremely well suited to the smaller garden. One of particular merit is the Paperbark Maple (*A. griseum*) which grows to a height of 40 ft. or so. The common name comes from the bark which peels

thinly to show the orange-red trunk underneath. The shapely leaves colour beautifully in autumn. Also good for autumn colour is *A. grosseri hersii* which has attractive white-lined bark and makes a tree up to 30 ft. in height. *A. negundo variegatum,* 25 ft. or so, is one of the best small trees for town gardens. The leaves are attractively variegated with white.

Amelanchier canadensis (Snowy Mespilus). The Snowy Mespilus pay a double dividend in the shape of a profusion of small white flowers which clothe the bare branches in April and leaves which turn brilliant red before they fall in autumn. It grows up to 30 ft. tall and as much across.

Arbor-vitae (see Thuja)

Arbutus unedo (Strawberry Tree). The evergreen Strawberry Tree is an attractive choice where colour and interest late in the year is desired. It should be planted in a sheltered position because of its late flowering. The panicles of white flowers are borne at the same time as the strawberry-like fruits in late autumn and are very decorative. The leaves are a splendid foil for these, being dark green and glossy. Unlike most ericaceous plants, *A. unedo*

Acer negundo variegatum is a handsome small tree with white variegated foliage and is well suited for planting in front gardens. Ornamental trees can add much to the appearance of a garden, especially when most of the other plants grown are of low stature

grows well in limy soils. It may reach 25 ft. or rather more in height but is more likely to be nearer 15 ft. tall.

Betula (Silver Birch). Although so common, and an offender in so much as it is a notorious soil robber, the birch in its numerous forms is a beautiful tree for many different settings. The colour of the bark and the lovely tracery of the bare branches in winter make this very much a tree of year-round interest. A popular variety is Young's Weeping Birch, *B. pendula youngii,* which makes a splendid lawn specimen. Another variety of *B. pendula* which has value for confined spaces is *fastigiata,* of erect habit rather like a Lombardy Poplar. Both these grow to 30 ft. or so in height. The Paper Birch, *B. papyrifera,* is a tree of twice this height with very white bark which is suitable for larger gardens.

Cedar (see Cedrus)

Cedrus (Cedar). It needs a large garden to even consider planting any of the cedars.

The beautiful Cedar of Lebanon, *C. libani,* needs no introduction, and mention must be made of *C. atlantica glauca,* an attractive variety of the Atlas Cedar with beautiful glaucous blue foliage and arching branches. Remember, though, that this tree can reach a height of around 100 ft. and have a spread of perhaps 50 ft. An open, sunny situation is desirable.

Chamaecyparis. This is an important genus for the intending planter, although most of them make large trees. The dwarf varieties do not concern us here. *C. lawsoniana,* the Lawson's Cypress, can reach a height of 100 ft. but many of its excellent varieties are of more modest stature. A few of special interest for their colouring are the pyramidal, glaucous green *allumii,* about 40 ft. tall; *lutea,* golden-foliaged, also about 40 ft. tall and called the Golden Lawson's Cypress; and Triomphe de Boskoop, about 50 ft. tall with handsome glaucous blue foliage and a pyramidal habit.

Two varieties of the Sarawa Cypress,

C. pisifera, with colourful foliage are *C. p. aurea* with golden leaves, and *C. p. plumosa argentea* with creamy-white tips to its shoots. Both are in the 30 to 35 ft. height range.

Cornus kousa. Shrub or tree? It is probably in between the two but that is not of importance. The main thing is that it has great charm in spring when it bears its showy white bracts in profusion. It eventually reaches a height of 20 ft. or so.

Crataegus (Thorn). There are various ornamental thorns which make good garden trees for open sunny positions, and one of the best is *C. oxyacantha coccinea plena*, Paul's Double Scarlet Thorn, which is a picture in May when carrying its mantle of rosy-red flowers. This, too, is a tree of about 20 ft. in height.

Cupressocyparis leylandii. Extremely fast growing and with a columnar habit, this cross between *Cupressus macrocarpa*

and *Chamaecyparis nootkatensis* is a fine specimen tree. It is a very good seaside conifer and does well on chalk. The foliage is dark green. It may reach a height of 60 ft.

Dawn Redwood (see Metasequoia)

Eucalyptus gunnii. This is probably the hardiest of the eucalypts and it is certainly worth growing, in well drained soil in warmer gardens, for its distinctive foliage. When mature—and it is a fast grower—it can make a tree 50 ft. tall. Juvenile specimens have glaucous blue and rounded leaves and adult trees, grey-green, long and narrow, pointed leaves.

False Acacia (see Robinia)

Flowering and Fruiting Crabs (see Malus)

Flowering Cherries, Plums, Peaches, Apricots and Almonds (see Prunus)

Golden Rain (see Laburnum)

Halesia monticola (Snowdrop Tree).

Left : In this garden, erect growing conifers—mainly forms of Chamaecyparis lawsoniana *(Lawson's Cypress)—are used as 'exclamation marks' in contrast to trees and shrubs of different shapes. Right : The erect* Prunus *Amanogawa, with semi-double pink flowers, makes an admirable focal point*

This can be grown as a shrub or small tree in lime-free soils. It is very beautiful indeed when carrying its bell-shaped white flowers in May.

Holly (see Ilex)

Ilex (Holly). The hollies usually grown are varieties of *I. aquifolium,* the Common Holly, and these include many with attractive variegated leaves. These are very accommodating plants which will grow well in the open or semi-shade. An excellent variety with silver variegation is the female *argenteo-marginata.* (It should be noted that both male and female varieties should be planted if good crops of berries are required.) For gold variegation an excellent variety is Madame Briot. Both these varieties will reach a height of around 20 ft.

Juniper (see Juniperus)

Juniperus (Juniper). A juniper which has considerable value from our point of view is the Irish Juniper, *J. communis hibernica.* This has a columnar habit and glaucous foliage and will eventually—for it is slow growing—reach a height of 10 to 15 ft. It likes lime in the soil.

Koelreuteria paniculata. This is an attractive, easily pleased tree which bears yellow flowers in summer and follows these with a display of bladder-like fruits. The foliage turns rich yellow in autumn. Although it does grow to 40 ft. tall, *K. paniculata* is more likely to be around 25 ft.

Laburnum (Golden Rain). The laburnums in their various forms are splendid trees for gardens of all sizes but one must be aware that the seeds are poisonous and can therefore be a hazard if there are young children in the family. Best of all is *L. vossii,* with long racemes of rich yellow flowers, which makes a tree of 15 to 25 ft. tall and is

a cross between the Common Laburnum, *L. vulgare,* and the Scotch Laburnum, *L. alpinum.* The common name Golden Rain is an apt description.

Lawson's Cypress (see Chamaecyparis)

Liquidambar (Sweet Gum). If you have the space, an open position and moist, loamy soil, there is no finer tree for rich crimson autumn colour than *L. styraciflua;* but with a height of 60 ft. and a spread almost as great it is not many gardeners who can indulge the luxury of growing this tree.

Magnolia. I shall mention only a few of the many lovely magnolias available, namely the popular 30 ft. tall *M. soulangiana,* which, with its numerous forms, is a superb town tree, among other things; *M. denudata,* a lovely species of about 25 ft. with white, cup-shaped flowers; and the evergreen *M. grandiflora* which grows well as a wall plant and bears fragrant, cup-shaped, creamy-white flowers from July to September. *M. soulangiana,* with large white flowers suffused with purple on the outside, provides a display in April and May and *M. denudata* comes into flower in early March. The latter may have its flowers damaged by frost.

All of the magnolias like a rich, well-drained soil, preferably free of lime.

Malus (Flowering and Fruiting Crabs). The flowering crabs make excellent trees for gardens of all sizes, many of them being in the 15 to 20 ft. height range although others reach 40 ft. or so. Of special interest are the deep crimson-flowered *M. lemoinei,* the pink-flowered *M. floribunda* (both about 25 ft. tall) and the fine fruiting crabs, Golden Hornet (yellow fruits), John Downie (yellow and red fruits) and Dartmouth (reddish-purple fruits). The crabs

The author by an island bed in his Shropshire garden which is planted with, among other hardy perennials, Achillea Coronation Gold and the geums Mrs Bradshaw, crimson, and Lady Stratheden, yellow. A merit of island beds is that they allow the plants to be viewed from all sides. Shrubs, too, are often grown in such borders in association with hardy perennials

The combination of colours in this border is especially pleasing to the eye. From the 'hot' Sweet William in the foreground, to the cool grey-leaved Stachys lanata, Canterbury Bells and delphiniums they create an impression of clear, fresh beauty, like a work from an artist's easel on which the paint has barely dried. This pattern of colour intensities can easily be repeated on a larger scale

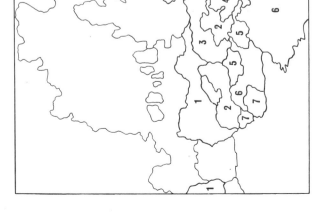

Key to Shrub Border
1. Syringa (white lilac)
2. Viburnum tomentosum mariesii
3. Pieris forrestii
4. Cytisus scoparius
5. Azaleas (deciduous hybrids)
6. Senecio laxifolius
7. Viburnum davidii

*A well-planned border of shrubs will provide colour
and interest over all four seasons. Three seasons are
covered in this section of border (see key) with lilac,
Viburnum tomentosum mariesii, pieris, cytisus and
azaleas providing a spring display, the grey-foliaged
Senecio laxifolius flowering in summer and Viburnum
davidii bearing blue berries in autumn*

The frothy beauty of flowering cherries is given added impact by providing them with a background of dark conifers. The effectiveness of many trees and shrubs can be enhanced by choosing background subjects of contrasting colouring

will grow well in any reasonable soil and in open positions.

Maple (see Acer)

Metasequoia glyptostroboides (Dawn Redwood). This very handsome fossil-age deciduous conifer, re-discovered in China in 1945, is certainly worth a place in many gardens. Its graceful habit and feathery foliage make it very attractive and the leaves turn a glorious shade of pink in autumn. It has not been in cultivation long enough to know its ultimate height, but this is likely to be 70 ft. or more and must be allowed for. It seems quite easily pleased and likes moist soil conditions.

Mountain Ash (see Sorbus)

Picea (Spruce). Many of the spruces are too large for garden planting but the slow-growing *P. pungens glauca*, the Blue Spruce, makes a handsome small tree with rich blue-grey glaucous foliage. Give this tree a sunny position.

Prunus. This genus includes the Flowering Cherries, Plums, Peaches, Apricots and Almonds, and other trees like the Cherry Laurel and Portugal Laurel. The value of the spring-flowering cherries, almonds and peaches is very great indeed, as their popularity bears witness. The flowering cherries will grow well in almost any reasonable garden soil but the almonds and peaches are better in a warm, sheltered position in a well-drained soil of rather better quality. Cherries of especial value, in my opinion, are the pure white, single-flowered Shiro-tae; the fastigiate, semi-double, pink Amanogawa (so useful with its narrow, up-right habit for confined spaces); the double, white Shirofugen, the double, rosy-pink Kanzan, and Pink Perfection, with double, carmine-pink flowers. Kanzan is taller than the others by at least 10 ft., growing up to 40 ft. in height. A lovely peach is *P. persica* Clara Meyer which only grows to about 15 ft. tall; an almond of merit is the double *P. communis roseo-plena,* with pale pink flowers. (See the remarks on colour combinations on p. 16.)

For autumn and winter flowering there is *P. subhirtella autumnalis,* which produces its semi-double white or pale pink flowers intermittently throughout the months from November to March. The purple-leaved *P. cerasifera atropurpurea* (better known as *P. pissardii*), with pink flowers, is very useful indeed for providing foliage contrasts in mixed planting schemes.

Robinia (False Acacia). The robinias, both trees and shrubs, are excellent plants for growing in towns, given any reasonable soil and a sunny position. The False Acacia, *R. pseudoacacia,* makes a tree 70 ft. or so in height and it has distinctive and very attractive pinnate leaves and white flowers which are borne in early summer. The variety *angustifolia* grows to only half this height and is also attractive.

Salix (Willow). The Golden Weeping Willow, *S. alba tristis* (syn. *S. a. vitellina pendula*), is a splendid garden tree where a suitable site can be provided. The attractions, apart from its habit, are the golden stems and bright green leaves. Its especial value for most gardens is that it is of smaller size than the Weeping Willow proper, *S. babylonica,* which is up to 50 ft. tall.

Silver Birch (see Betula)

Snowdrop Tree (see Halesia)

Snowy Mespilus (see Amelanchier)

Sorbus (Mountain Ash and Whitebeam). The Mountain Ash, *S. aucuparia,* and its varieties, are suitable trees for town or country gardens, with attractive flowers, fruits and fern-like foliage. An especially good variety for autumn display is *edulis,* which has larger fruits than the others. A noteworthy whitebeam is *S. aria lutescens* which is easily distinguished by the greyish coloured hairs which cover the leaves and give the tree such a handsome appearance.

Spruce (see Picea)

Strawberry Tree (see Arbutus)

Sweet Gum (see Liquidambar)

Taxus (Yew). The English Yew, *T. baccata,* is another tree which needs no introduction, and even bearing in mind its slow rate of growth it is still very valuable for garden planting, where space is available. Where space is limited the Irish Yew, *T. b. fastigiata*—which is also available in a golden-leaved form, *aurea*—is an excellent proposition with its upright habit and height of about 15 ft. or so.

Thorn (see Crataegus)

Thuja (Arbor-vitae). The variegated form of the Western Arbor-vitae, *T. plicata zebrina,* with its foliage banded in green and yellow, is an especially showy member of this genus of conifers. Height up to 30 ft.

Whitebeam (see Sorbus)

Willow (see Salix)

Yew (see Taxus)

CHAPTER EIGHT

Climbing and Wall Plants for Colour

WALLS and fences can easily be made attractive by clothing their nakedness with suitable climbing plants whose flowers or leaves will, in their season, provide much colour and interest. At the same time one is increasing the scope of one's gardening interests. Numerous shrubs which are not climbing plants at all are excellent for growing against walls. A sheltered wall may provide just the warm corner for a favourite plant that would not survive in an exposed place in the garden, yet how often we see gardens where the best use is not made of such opportunities. The period of interest can also be extended by planting several different climbers in close proximity to each other.

One must naturally try and match the colour of brick walls with the colours of the plants to be grown. This factor can be overlooked quite easily—as I know well. The neutral colour of stone means that it mixes well with almost anything.

Wherever climbers and wall shrubs are planted they will become permanent features and once planted they should not be disturbed. This means that we must be sure that we choose the right position in the first place and that the soil is thoroughly prepared before planting. There is little

that can be done in this respect after planting other than to give a top dressing of compost, peat or old manure in the autumn or early spring, depending on the plants' requirements.

I mention choosing the right place for I have seen camellias, which are not climbers, of course, but are most decorative wall plants, planted in full sun against a south-facing wall because it was imagined that they were tender. The result was that they started to shrivel, but fortunately they were transplanted before it was too late.

SOME RECOMMENDATIONS

Abutilon. In the milder parts of the country, the dainty *A. megapotamicum* is well worth trying in a south- or west-facing corner, for although it is not a true climber it can be trained against a wall. It grows about 6 ft. tall and bears a succession of pendant red and yellow lantern-shaped flowers with prominent brownish anthers from June to October. This shrub is a native of Brazil and should be protected in severe weather with what we used to call Archangel mats, or sacking. West Country gardeners may smile at this suggestion, but many of us have more rigorous conditions to contend with in winter, and, even worse, in late spring.

Batchelor's Buttons (see Kerria)

Bilderdyckia (Polygonum) baldschuanicum (Russian Vine). The very rampant Russian Vine, *B. baldschuanicum* until recently known as *Polygonum baldschuanicum,* might be described as a plant in a hurry. Certainly it is unsurpassed for providing cover over a large area quickly. An unsightly shed, a large bare wall or similar structure will soon be lost behind its leafy mantle. From July to autumn, too, this deciduous climber bears freely its pinkish-white flowers which are not without their beauty. Altogether this is a useful shrub to remember—but only plant it where it can be given its head and the site is in keeping with its growth potential.

Camellia. I have already referred to the widespread misconception that camellias are tender, although I am sure that more and more gardeners are realising that this is not so. The many varieties of the evergreen *C. japonica* are perfectly hardy, although their blooms are liable to damage by spring frosts. What they must have is a lime-free, cool, moist soil and they should be planted so that they are shaded from the early morning sun, which is so damaging to the blooms after a frosty night. A west- or north-facing aspect is the best. Where a camellia does get a good deal of sun it will need ample water in the summer and a good mulch to conserve moisture in the soil.

Chaenomeles (Japanese Quince). See description on p. 49.

Campsis radicans (Trumpet Creeper). The Trumpet Creeper, a native of North America and formerly known as *Tecoma* and *Bignonia*, is a handsome, vigorous climber for a warm wall in full sun. As a young plant it may need protection during severe weather, but once established it is reasonably hardy. The large trumpet-shaped scarlet and orange flowers are freely produced in August and September. It climbs to a height of 20 ft. or more by means of its aerial roots. The Oriental species, *C. grandiflora* (syn. *C. chinensis*), has orange and red blooms but it is not so self-supporting as *C. radicans.*

Chimonanthus praecox (Winter Sweet). A most lovely shrub for growing against a warm south- or west-facing wall is *C. praecox* (syn. *C. fragrans*). This bears pale yellow flowers with purple centres on the bare branches in December and January. The petals have a distinctive waxy appearance. The fragrance is such that just a small flowering shoot left in a room overnight will fill the air with its sweetness. There is a beautiful clear primrose yellow variety, *luteus,* which comes into flower in February. Both will eventually make shrubs up to 10 ft. tall and across, if well suited. They like best a rather light loam which is retentive of moisture.

Clematis. These glorious climbing plants are justly popular and there are a great many species and hybrids available from specialist growers—far more different varieties, I am sure, than is generally appreciated. They are grown in pots by nurserymen and are best planted in October and November or in spring. The soil should be moist but at the same time well drained and the lower parts of the plants' stems should be shaded from direct sun.

Clematis are hardy and it is a mistake to plant them against hot walls unless the roots and lower parts of the plants are reasonably cool and moist. Which to plant is a matter of personal preference, but where a quick grower is required to cover an old shed or tree then I suggest *C. montana* which is a mass of star-like white flowers

Cotoneaster horizontalis is a valuable wall shrub which is especially well suited for planting under windows. Its attractions include its flat habit and the red berries which are borne in autumn

in May and June. There are also one or two pink forms of this species, *rubens* being one which also has attractive bronze-purple leaves in the spring. Another strong grower which will make annual growths of 10 to 15 ft. is *C. spooneri,* which bears large, pure white flowers with yellow centres in June.

Best of all is the violet-purple hybrid *C. jackmanii* which flowers freely from July to September or even later. Other lovely large-flowered hybrids include the clear pink Comtesse de Bouchaud; the robustly growing, carmine-red Ville de Lyon; the pinkish-mauve Marcel Moser, which has petals marked with a carmine bar; and Lasurstern, purplish-blue with prominent gold stamens, which makes a grand show in May and June and again in September. Another charming variety that flowers in the spring and the autumn is the large, pale mauve-pink Nelly Moser which has a deep carmine bar on each of its petals.

Then there is the evergreen *C. armandii* which starts to flower in late March and bears its white blooms in clusters. The leaves of this species are leathery, pointed and quite different from those of the deciduous varieties. It does best on a sheltered wall as long as the roots are kept moist.

Cotoneaster. The deciduous *C. horizontalis* with its flat, herring-bone-like habit is a splendid wall shrub, decorative for many months of the year but especially so when carrying its crop of red berries in autumn. Reaching a height of 2 to 3 ft. and having a spread of 8 to 10 ft. it is well suited for a position under a window or against a low wall which it is desired to screen. The low-growing *C. microphyllus,* an evergreen with crimson berries, is also useful for growing over retaining walls.

Escallonia macrantha. This evergreen species makes a satisfactory wall shrub. Its habit is rounded and it reaches a height of about 10 ft. Its light crimson flowers are borne from June to September.

Euonymus. Often used as a ground-cover

[63]

plant, the evergreen *E. radicans* will support itself by aerial roots if planted against a wall, either in sun or shade. The variety Silver Queen is more decorative than the species and its broad leaves have pleasing silver variegation.

Firethorn (see Pyracantha)

Forsythia suspensa. The distinctive *F. suspensa* with pendulous habit and bright yellow flowers is a good choice for a north or east wall where a shrub of about 10 to 12 ft. is needed. It flowers in March-early April.

Garrya elliptica. Already described on p. 44, *G. elliptica* in its male form is another good plant for a north or east wall.

Hedera (Ivy). It is the current enthusiasm for house plants which has brought the ornamental ivies to the forefront and very attractive these can be in carefully chosen positions. Two outstanding varieties are *H. canariensis variegata,* a handsome form of the Canary Island Ivy with large, rounded, dark green leaves bordered with

silver-white, and *H. colchica dentata variegata* whose large soft green leaves are broadly margined with pale gold. Both grow to a height of 10 ft. or so. Many other varieties with leaves of different shapes and sizes are available and will be found listed in good shrub catalogues. All have the merit of growing well with any aspect.

Honeysuckle (see Lonicera)

Hydrangea petiolaris. The self-clinging climbing hydrangea *H. petiolaris* is recommended for a north- or east-facing wall or for growing on a tree to a height of 20 ft. or more. This deciduous species bears large, flat heads of white flowers in June and July. Not so reliably hardy as *H. petiolaris* is the deciduous *H. anomala,* with leaves pleasingly curled and glossy when young. This also is self-clinging and it bears creamy-white flat flowers in June and July.

Itea ilicifolia. If the kerria referred to next is one of the most ubiquitous of shrubs, the evergreen *I. ilicifolia* is the opposite. This

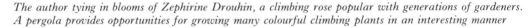

The author tying in blooms of Zephirine Drouhin, a climbing rose popular with generations of gardeners. A pergola provides opportunities for growing many colourful climbing plants in an interesting manner

handsome shrub bears long pendulous racemes of catkin-like greenish-white, fragrant flowers in late summer. It should be planted against a south- or west-facing wall and does best in a loamy soil or sandy peat with plenty of moisture. Once established it makes quite quick growth, attaining a height of about 8 ft.

Ivy (see Hedera)

Jasmine (see Jasminum)

Jasminum (Jasmine). For descriptions of those two excellent climbers, *J. officinale* and *J. nudiflorum,* see pp. 50 and 52 respectively.

Kerria. The fact that Batchelor's Buttons, *K. japonica pleniflora,* is one of the most frequently seen garden shrubs should not make one pass it over when drawing up planting schemes. It is a pretty shrub in April and May with its mass of ball-like orange-yellow flowers borne on thin, arching stems, and its popularity is a measure of its good natured acceptance of widely differing conditions. In fact, this deciduous shrub grows well given any aspect and is as happy against a wall or fence as when it is grown as a free-standing specimen. It usually reaches a height of about 10 ft.

Lonicera (Honeysuckle). Among the most lovely, informal climbers are the honeysuckles. Two deliciously fragrant deciduous varieties are the Early Dutch (*L. periclymenum belgica*), which flowers in June and July, and the late Dutch (*L. p. serotina*), which follows in August and September. Both have reddish-purple flowers, yellow within. They may be planted with any aspect, but a south-facing wall might prove too hot, at any rate in the south of England.

The evergreen *L. japonica halliana* will also succeed given any aspect and in sun or shade. It is quick growing and bears fragrant flowers—soft creamy-yellow, fading to ochre—from June to October. The individual flowers are small but are neatly arranged in pairs along the whole length of the current year's growth, which accounts for the continuity of flower. It can become untidy, but if the twiggy shoots are cut out in March this will keep it in reasonable order. This is an admirable plant to grow on a trellis or porch.

The large-flowered, deciduous *L. tellmanniana* makes a great show in June and July and does best on a semi-shaded, west-facing wall. Unfortunately, its rich yellow flowers flushed with red are not scented—but in the garden as elsewhere one cannot always have everything. Another evergreen honeysuckle for planting with any aspect is *L. japonica aureo-reticulata* which has oval leaves veined golden-yellow. This is a good climber to plant near the front door of the house where all-season interest is a particular asset.

Parthenocissus. The well-known Virginia Creeper *P. quinquefolia* (syn. *Vitis quinquefolia*) is seen at its best when growing up a tall tree with its long trailing growths of fresh green, three- or five-lobed leaves swaying in the breeze. In autumn the leaves turn a spectacular scarlet and orange. It is self-clinging on a wall but it does require ample space or it may grow into guttering and become too exuberant around windows. Outstanding for autumn colour and also a strong grower is *P. tricuspidata* (syn. *Ampelopsis veitchii*) and *P. henryana* (syn. *Vitis henryana*) which will soon cover a large wall. The leaves are variegated pink and white and the characteristic is more pronounced when the plant is growing in partial shade, although it is quite happy in full sun. In autumn the leaves turn brilliant red.

Left : The tall-growing climber Schizophragma hydrangeoides *makes luxuriant growth and in July bears small creamy-white flowers surrounded by pale yellow bracts. Right : The wisterias are superb wall shrubs and provide a spectacular display in early summer*

Passiflora caerulea (Passion Flower). In the South and West where a sheltered, sunny wall can be offered, a showy climber is the Passion Flower, *P. caerulea*. The fragrant flowers, up to 4 in. across, are distinctive in appearance and a lovely amalgam of white and blue shades. There is also an ivory-white variety, Constance Elliott. The flowers are borne from June to September.

Passion Flower (see Passiflora)

Pyracantha (Firethorn). For description of these very useful wall shrubs turn to p. 52.

Rosa (Rose). If we want to introduce vertical colour into our gardens we have,

of course, a treasure chest of good things in the climbing and rambling roses. I shall content myself now with mentioning a few of these roses which I consider especially noteworthy. The catalogues of rose specialists will provide information on many more which may be nearer your own tastes and requirements. The range of offerings is so great that, when making a choice, personal preferences must come into the picture more than they do with most shrubs.

For house walls the most suitable roses are the Climbers, which include the climbing sports of hybrid teas and floribundas and climbing shrub roses like the grand old rose-pink, fragrant Zephirine Drouhin and the primrose yellow Mermaid, also fragrant and with showy deep yellow stamens which, once established, provides a lovely display of colour from early summer to autumn. Among Ramblers, so excellent for pergolas, fences, pillars and arches, names like Paul's Scarlet Climber, Alberic Barbier (yellow in the bud and then creamy-white), American Pillar (rose with a white eye) and Albertine (deep pink marked salmon in the bud and later coppery-pink) are legion.

Rose (see Rosa)

Russian Vine (see Bilderdyckia)

Schizophragma. A handsome plant which resembles *Hydrangea petiolaris* (described on p. 64) is burdened with the name *Schizophragma hydrangeoides*. The generic name refers to the curious splitting of the seed capsules and the specific name to the hydrangea-like flowers. It is, however, the pale yellow bracts surrounding the small creamy-white flowers in July which are the chief attraction of this deciduous shrub. It will grow in semi-shade or sun, but usually flowers more freely in sunny positions. It will climb to 20 ft. or more once established.

Stauntonia. The evergreen, twining *Stauntonia hexaphylla*, which grows vigorously in milder districts, also reaches a height of 20 ft. or more. It has large leaves and white, tinged violet, fragrant flowers, and it deserves to be better known and more often grown.

Trumpet Creeper (see Campsis)

Virginia Creeper (see Parthenocissus)

Vitis. The genus *Vitis* includes the magnificent *V. coignetiae,* a strong-growing species with leaves often as much as a foot across. These colour superbly in the autumn. For covering a wall facing in any direction or adorning a large tree this vine can be thoroughly recommended — but it needs space to do it justice. There is magnificent autumn colour, too, from *V. vinifera* Brandt, a variety of the edible grape, whose leaves turn to lovely shades of red and orange at that time of the year. *V. v. purpurea*, called the Teinturier Grape, is also notable in this respect for the claret red foliage turns to a particularly striking shade of purple in the autumn. Both varieties need a warm south- or west-facing wall and will reach a height of 10 ft. or more.

Winter Sweet (see Chimonanthus)

Wisteria. The wisterias are perhaps the best known of all climbing plants for their striking trails of flowers can hardly be overlooked in early summer. Superb wall plants, they are also much used, of course, for pergolas, pillars and similar structures and are sometimes grown as free-standing specimens on a short 'leg'. The most usually grown species is *W. sinensis,* a Chinese wisteria with mauve flowers borne on racemes up to a foot in length. Also handsome and popular is *W. floribunda macrobotrys* which has bluish-purple flowers borne on racemes up to 3 ft. long.

CHAPTER NINE

Hedging Plants for Colour

MOST gardens have a hedge of some sort to form a boundary, to provide a wind-break or maybe to afford some privacy. It is a permanent feature, yet so often little thought is given to make a hedge a really attractive and colourful part of the garden. There is, nowadays, a wide range of plants which are suitable for this purpose, either for a high hedge or for a low hedge forming a division within the garden or alongside a path. For the last mentioned purpose, of course, fragrant lavender has much to commend it.

Privet which was planted in suburban gardens in vast quantities years ago is deadly dull and impoverishes the soil so thoroughly that it should never be planted in a small garden. While the golden form is more cheerful looking it is an equally hungry plant. As I have already said a hedge is a permanent feature, so give considerable thought to the subject before deciding which plant will be most suitable to meet your requirements, always bearing in mind the kind of soil available and the aspect.

PREPARING THE SOIL

The next thing is to prepare the soil thoroughly, for once the hedge is planted there is not much that can be done, other than an occasional top dressing with leaf-mould or peat, if it should prove necessary. If the depth of soil permits it should be dug to a depth of about 18 in., but the subsoil must not be brought to the surface. Dig a trench, at least 2 ft. wide, and having taken out the top soil, break up the subsoil with a fork to ensure good drainage, before replacing the top soil. When this soil is being put back into the trench, work in some well-rotted farmyard manure, if obtainable, or failing this some hop manure and garden compost. Bonemeal, applied at the rate of 4 oz. to the square yard, is also a good slow-acting fertiliser. Quick-acting fertilisers should be avoided where hedges are concerned. If the soil is deficient in lime then fork in, or scatter on the surface, hydrated lime at the rate of up to 4 oz. to the square yard. Remember, however, that such plants as the common, purple *Rhododendron ponticum,* which makes quite a good evergreen hedge, require a lime-free soil.

There should be a gap of at least some weeks—the longer the better—between the preparation of the soil and planting so that the soil has time to settle.

PLANTING

I prefer to plant deciduous hedges in the

autumn, although any time from mid-October to mid-March is quite suitable, as long as the soil is in workable condition. Evergreen hedges are best planted in September or October, or from mid-March to early May. One must remember that evergreens never cease to lose moisture through their leaves and they are, therefore, in a particularly vulnerable position until they have established themselves in their new home. Where evergreens are planted in the spring and the weather becomes dry and warm, the plants will benefit from a spray overhead with water in the evenings until they have made new roots and become established. This attention has saved many a gap in a young hedge and is well worth the effort. Cupressus and yew often give the most trouble in this respect. If a polythene bag is placed over each specimen for a week or two after planting this will prevent many losses.

Should there be a long dry spell of weather it will be necessary to water the plants thoroughly at the roots. Mulching with moist peat or compost around the plants will help to conserve moisture. Grass cuttings may also be used for this purpose so long as the lawn has not been dressed recently with selective weed-killer.

SIZE OF PLANTS

Frequently a hedge is required to provide a screen as quickly as possible, and for this reason tall plants are ordered. This, however, may not achieve the objective for such plants take longer to become established and may not have good fibrous roots, unless they have been regularly transplanted while growing in the nursery. Plants which have not been transplanted will probably have woody roots, and, while they may be cheaper in the first instance, should be avoided because they will take much longer to 'get away' and losses can be considerable,

so that they may turn out to be an expensive proposition. Hedging plants are quoted by the 100 or by the dozen, the more unusual varieties at the dozen rate.

Some hedging plants, such as pyracantha and broom (cytisus), are grown in pots by nurserymen and can therefore be planted at almost any time so long as the ground is not frozen, and it is not high summer. Such plants cost more, of course, than those which are grown in large quantities in the open ground.

There are many good hedge plants, but some will not do well in all places. I have, therefore, made three lists, namely for town gardens, chalk soils, and the seaside, which are the most difficult situations. People who live in easier places should remember that shrubs for town gardens will grow in the country, and those for chalk soils will grow on lime-free soils, but those listed for the seaside will not necessarily grow inland, because frosts are generally much worse inland than by the sea. For ease of reference I have sometimes included the same plant in more than one list.

FOR TOWN GARDENS

The following are all useful plants for this purpose:

Barberry (see Berberis)

Beech (see Fagus)

Berberis (Barberry). Three good evergreen hedging plants are *B. darwinii,* with orange-yellow flowers in April-May; *B. gagnepainii,* yellow, which flowers in the second half of May; and *B. stenophylla,* orange-yellow and April-May-flowering. These will make hedges of 8 ft., 4 ft. and 10 ft. respectively.

Cotoneaster. The scarlet-berried *C. simonsii* with silvery-grey bark makes a good hedge of about 5 ft. in height.

Euonymus. The evergreen *Euonymus japonicus,* except in its interesting variegated forms, is not a very exciting shrub but it stands up well to atmospheric pollution and will provide a screen some 10 ft. in height. This is not a shrub for cold gardens, but is excellent in coastal areas.

Fagus (Beech). The popular Beech, *Fagus sylvatica,* is almost as good as an evergreen for hedging for the leaves, which turn a lovely bronze colour in autumn, remain on the plants throughout the winter.

Firethorn (see Pyracantha)

Flowering Currant (see Ribes)

Forsythia. As a hedging plant, forsythia can be extremely attractive in spring. Chestnut fencing, for example, can be masked successfully with this shrub and the best-known variety undoubtedly is *F. intermedia spectabilis,* a rich deep yellow in colour, which will make a hedge up to 8 or 9 ft. tall.

Hebe. This is the correct generic name for the evergreen shrubby veronicas, but they are most often found listed in catalogues under the latter name. The hardiest is *H. traversii* which bears white flowers in June. This will make a hedge up to 6 ft. tall.

Holly (see Ilex)

Honeysuckle (see Lonicera)

Ilex (Holly). There are numerous varieties of the evergreen Common Holly, *I. aquifolium,* which make good hedge plants and screens up to 20 ft. tall if necessary. The elegant but slow-growing gold and silver forms, like *I. a.* Golden King and *I. a.* Silver Queen, are to be recommended.

Laurustinus (see Viburnum)

Lonicera (Honeysuckle). The small-leaved evergreen *L. nitida* makes a neat formal hedge when carefully trimmed to a wedge-shaped top, this last being necessary to avoid the hedge being broken down by the weight of snow in winter. For a hedge with a height of about 4 ft. it has much to commend it, but remember that it can be damaged by severe weather.

New Zealand Daisy Bush (see Olearia)

Olearia haastii (New Zealand Daisy Bush). The tough, rounded leaves of this evergreen are grey beneath and it bears clusters of white flowers in July. This also makes a hedge of about 4 ft.

Osmarea burkwoodii. This handsome evergreen with dark green foliage and fragrant white flowers in May makes a hedge about 5 ft. tall. It is certainly worth considering, especially if a good hedging plant is wanted which is rather out of the common run of things.

Pyracantha (Firethorn). The evergreen pyracanthas, so overplanted as wall shrubs in years past, are, of course, splendid shrubs and they make excellent informal hedges (if clipped few berries are borne). Best known is *P. coccinea lalandii* with bright red berries and *P. atlantioides* which will make fine hedges of 10 ft. or so in height, if required.

Rhododendron. Some of the rhododendrons make good hedging plants for lime-free soils. The common rhododendron, *R. ponticum* (height 7 to 15 ft.), grows well in towns and so do some of the named hybrids, which will make a most colourful screen but will also cost considerably more to buy.

Ribes sanguineum (Flowering Currant). The flowering currant and varieties such as King Edward VII make attractive hedges of 8 ft. or more in height within a garden,

Lavender makes an attractive low hedge for sunny positions and well-drained soils. The Old English Lavender grows 4 ft. tall and there is a range of varieties down to 1 ft. tall with flowers in colours from purple to lavender, lilac and white

but are not thick enough for a boundary hedge. The rosy-red flowers of *R. sanguineum* appear in April and have a delightful foil in the bright green leaves. King Edward VII has deep crimson flowers.

Viburnum. An evergreen viburnum which is excellent for hedge making is the popular Laurustinus, *V. tinus*. This makes a hedge up to 10 ft. tall and bears attractive clusters of white flowers—pink in the bud stage—during winter and spring. The leaves are dark green.

FOR CHALK SOILS

Beech (see Fagus)

Berberis. Numerous species and hybrids, both evergreen and deciduous, are useful for this purpose, including *B. darwinii, B. wilsonae, B. stenophylla* and *B. thunbergii.*

Box (see Buxus)

Buxus (Box). The common box, *B. sempervirens,* is a fine evergreen hedge plant for chalky soils, providing screens of 8 ft. or a little more in height. There is a colour-ful gold-variegated variety named *aurea maculata.* For low hedges of 3 ft. or less in height there is *B. s. elegantissima,* which has leaves edged with silver, and the Edging Box, *B. suffruticosa.*

Chaenomeles (Japanese Quince). The numerous varieties of *Chaenomeles speciosa* will provide hedges of heights from 4 to 8 ft. Especially attractive are the 5 ft. tall Knap Hill Scarlet, with flowers of orange-scarlet and the apple-blossom pink Moerloesii, which grows to a height of about 6 ft. Prune back the shoots after flowering otherwise the plants are liable to sprawl.

Cherry Plum (see Prunus)

Cotoneaster. Of the numerous evergreen and deciduous cotoneasters suitable for this purpose I would mention *C. lacteus,* an evergreen species which bears white flowers in June and red berries later and makes a hedge of about 10 ft., and the semi-evergreen *C. simonsii* with showy dark leaves which bears its red berries freely in autumn. This makes a hedge of up to 5 ft.

[71]

Escallonia. Deservedly popular as seaside shrubs, the hardiest of this genus of evergreens is *E. langleyensis* with light crimson flowers but none of them are reliable except at the seaside. Escallonias are best grown as an informal hedge or windbreak so that the arching sprays of flowers can be seen to full advantage. *E. langleyensis* makes a hedge of up to 10 ft., and varieties like the deep red C. F. Ball and the pink Donard Seedling, screens of about 6 ft. in height.

Fagus (Beech). *Fagus sylvatica* is a good standby on chalky soil and the absence of flowers is made up for by the attractiveness of its leaves—fresh green in spring and bronze throughout the winter. It makes a hedge 5 to 10 ft. tall.

Firethorn (see Pyracantha)

Fuchsia. Hardy fuchsias, notably *F. magellanica riccartonii,* with red and purple flowers, make charming hedges, especially within a garden, in mild districts. Height 4 to 8 ft.

Guelder Rose (see Viburnum)

Japanese Quince (see Chaenomeles)

Laurustinus (see Viburnum)

Lavender (see Lavandula)

Lavender Cotton (see Santolina)

Lavandula (Lavender). Lavender makes a delightful small hedge for a sunny position and well-drained soil. There are several varieties of the evergreen *L. spica,* the Old English Lavender, and Nana Munstead Dwarf is one of the most compact, growing about 1 ft. high. This has deep lavender-blue flowers.

Lilac (see Syringa)

Myrobalan (see Prunus)

Prunus. The Myrobalan or Cherry Plum (*P. cerasifera*) makes a quick-growing hedge up to about 10 ft. and the small white flowers are attractive in spring. The varieties *atropurpurea* (syn. *P. c. pissardii*) and *nigra* have dark purple leaves and make a striking background for white-flowered hardy herbaceous plants.

Pyracantha (Firethorn). The evergreen pyracanthas also make a stout hedge and when grown informally, that is not clipped too vigorously, the berries—orange, red or yellow, depending on which species or variety is planted—are freely borne and are most colourful in autumn. Plant pot-grown specimens about $1\frac{1}{2}$ to 2 ft. in height. These make a hedge 4 to 8 ft. tall.

Rosemary (see Rosmarinus)

Rosmarinus (Rosemary). On a light, well-drained soil the aromatic *R. officinalis* makes a delightful evergreen hedge up to 6 ft. tall. Trim after the blue flowers have faded in June.

Santolina. The evergreen Lavender Cotton, *S. chamaecyparissus* (syn. *S. incana*) has silvery-grey leaves covered with white felt and during the summer bears yellow, button-like flowers. It makes an effective hedge for bordering a path, growing $1\frac{1}{2}$ to 2 ft. tall.

Senecio. If something taller with silvery-grey foliage than the santolina mentioned above is required, then plant *S. laxifolius* (syn. *S. greyi*) which grows 3 ft. tall and also provides an evergreen screen. The leathery leaves are covered with grey felt on the underside. In June and July it bears yellow, daisy-like flowers.

Snowball Tree (see Viburnum)

Syringa (Lilac). Where a big, fast-growing screen is required the lilac, *Syringa vulgaris,* is most decorative. There are single and double varieties in shades of deep purple, mauve, rosy-pink and white, and, of course, the fragrance is enchanting. When grown as an informal screen—up to 10 ft. tall—the flower heads should be removed before they start to seed, at the same time thinning out weak growths. A hedge of this kind may be expensive initially but it makes an admirable, very hardy and lasting screen.

Viburnum. The Laurustinus, *Viburnum tinus,* does as well on chalk as it does in town gardens (see p. 71). The Guelder Rose, *V. opulus,* makes a hedge up to 10 ft. and bears flat heads of white flowers in June and red berries in autumn. The foliage also takes on pleasing autumn tints. The Snowball Tree, *V. opulus sterile,* can also be planted as a hedge and bears white balls of bloom in June. It makes a hedge of about 5 to 6 ft. in height.

FOR SEASIDE GARDENS

Having a garden near the sea can be pleasant but it also presents problems. Frost is not usually one of these, but gales and salt spray can play havoc with many plants so they must be chosen with care, particularly where hedges are concerned as shrubs used for this purpose will probably be exposed to all the elements. The following should prove satisfactory and provide colour or a pleasant foil for colour:

Atriplex halimus (Tree Purslane). This shrub is semi-evergreen with silver-grey leaves and though it cannot be described as colourful it withstands spray and gales like a seagull, and provides a useful foil and protection for tender and/or more colourful plants within the garden. Planted in a double row it will form a useful windbreak 6 to 8 ft. high.

Cherry Plum (see Prunus)

Escallonia. *Escallonia macrantha* is an especially good seaside shrub and will provide an evergreen screen up to 10 ft. high. It bears bright red flowers in June and July and has large glossy green leaves. Hybrids of this species also thrive by the sea.

Euonymus. Planted extensively along the south coast of England, *E. japonicus* has dark glossy green leaves that are usually unharmed by spray. The gold and silver forms, like *ovatus aureus* and *macrophyllus albus,* are more decorative than the type. All these make hedges up to 8 ft. tall.

Fuchsia. A fuchsia that is often grown for hedging purposes near the sea in milder areas, is the red and purple flowered *F. magellanica riccartonii.* It makes a hedge of up to 8 ft.

Gorse (see Ulex)

Hebe. The hebes, or shrubby veronicas (see p. 70 for description), provide a useful screen throughout the year.

Hippophae rhamnoides (Sea Buckthorn). This is another useful windbreak hedge plant with silvery leaves and bark and orange berries in autumn. To obtain berries, though, some male plants must be planted with female specimens.

Hydrangea. In the West Country, with its moist atmosphere, *H. macrophylla* and its many colourful named varieties flower exuberantly. These will form hedges some 6 ft. or so tall.

Laurustinus (see Viburnum)

Myrobalan (see Prunus)

New Zealand Daisy Bush (see Olearia)

Olearia haastii (New Zealand Daisy Bush). This shrub (see p. 70) will thrive in gardens which are more exposed than those suited for the hydrangeas mentioned above and is undeterred by wind.

Roses of many types make excellent hedges, especially as partitions within a garden. Shown above is Rosa gallica versicolor *(*Rosa Mundi*), a shrub rose of unusual charm with pale crimson flowers, splashed with pink and white*

Prunus. The Myrobalan or Cherry Plum, *P. cerasifera* (see p. 72), grows well by the sea.

Sea Buckthorn (see Hippophae)

Tamarisk (see Tamarix)

Tamarix (Tamarisk). The deciduous tamarisks are especially associated with seaside conditions, the two best known ones being the pink *T. tetrandra* and the rosy-pink *T. pentandra*. Both make good windbreaks of 10 ft. or more in height.

Tree Purslane (see Atriplex)

Ulex (Gorse). The tough, colourful gorse, *Ulex europaeus,* makes a splendid evergreen barrier of up to 5 ft. in height and the long-lasting flowers have a refreshing honeyed fragrance on sunny days. The double-flowered variety *plenus* makes a wonderful display in April and May with its rich golden-yellow blooms and makes a better, more dense screen than the type.

Viburnum tinus (Laurustinus). This evergreen winter-flowering shrub, already described on p. 71, provides a useful screen for the whole of the year.

ROSE HEDGES

A hedge of roses within a garden, say to screen the vegetable garden, can be most effective during the summer. In addition, some of the shrub roses have colourful hips in the autumn. The choice is wide and one's selection can be made from any good rose catalogue. Floribunda roses are also colourful and three that are admirable for hedging purposes are Queen Elizabeth, Masquerade and Border King. The planting of briars such as *canina, laxa* and *multiflora,* which are offered for this purpose, is not to be recommended.

Senecio laxifolius is one of those shrubs which has continuous rather than seasonal interest for its handsome evergreen grey-felted leaves are pleasing to the eye at all times. The cheery daisy flowers are borne at about mid-summer. It grows 3ft. or so tall and as much as 6ft. wide and is suited for many sunny situations

Pieris forrestii is a superb shrub which also pays a double dividend for in addition to its white lily-of-the-valley-like flowers it bears, as shown above, young shoots of red colouring. This striking combination makes this evergreen one of the choicest for spring display, but it must have a lime-free soil and a sheltered position. It grows up to 7ft. tall

If familiarity breeds contempt then we should, perhaps, be contemptuous of the Laburnum, or Golden Rain to give it its very apt common name. Not many of us would be so foolish, though, to so summarily dismiss such a splendid ornamental tree, suitable alike for large and small gardens. The only note of caution to sound is to warn parents of young children

This glorious collection of ornamental trees and shrubs at Grayswood Hill Haslemere, Surrey, photographed in all their autumnal finery, is an object lesson in the colour grouping which can be arranged by clever planning and foresight. The large trees in the background demand more space than

CHAPTER TEN

Roses for Display

SOME plants look well in mixture, but not roses. There is too much variation in height and habit for them to be really satisfactory in assortment. The most effective way to plant roses is in good blocks of one variety with adjacent varieties carefully chosen to give a pleasing harmony or contrast. Of course, in small gardens large blocks are impossible, but even if there is only room for a dozen roses all told I would sooner see these in one, two or at the very most three varieties, than all different.

Before the advent of vermilion and vivid orange varieties there was really not much problem about colour association with roses, but nowadays varieties like Super Star and Orange Sensation can clash with some crimson, red and pink roses. White can be the salvation here as with so many other difficult flower colours. A bed of Iceberg behind a bed of Orange Sensation will show it off to perfection and no one can be offended by it. Some of the softer yellows can also be used, and also coppery-pinks, but these need more care and it would be wise to get cut flowers of the fancied varieties, and try arranging them in the same vase before deciding to plant them side by side in the garden. Though roses can be moved even several years after planting if it turns out that rearrange-ment is necessary, they do not take it so kindly as some other shrubs—rhododen-drons, for example, azaleas and camellias. So it is wise to get things right at the outset.

Best Type for Colour Display

When planning primarily for colour dis-play the floribunda roses are to be pre-ferred to the hybrid teas, because they produce far more flowers at a time. Good hybrid teas will give enough flowers for a week or so in June or early July to make a fairly solid display, but thereafter their flower production is liable to be patchy.

This is even more true of climbers, and even those that are said to be continuous flowering produce as a rule only a scattering of blooms at a time after their main flush. For real colour effect it may be better to rely on varieties such as Albertine, Chap-lin's Pink Climber and Dr Van Fleet that really do give one tremendous display, and then to rely on other climbers to keep the colour going later.

Variations in Habit

One point seldom discussed is the habit of roses. As I have already said, it varies a great deal between varieties and can make or mar the effect of a bed. Ideally roses should branch freely and make plenty of foliage so that they cover the ground well at all times when they are in leaf. A lot of varieties fulfil these requirements, but there are plenty which are sparse in habit and in foliage, and some which need to be planted more closely than others because of their erect habit.

HYBRID TEA ROSES

Pink

Ballet. This has large shapely bluey-pink flowers of good shape. It is of medium height and gives a fine display.

Gavotte. This medium-sized variety has shapely rose-pink flowers with a paler reverse. It is quite easy to place in planting schemes.

Grace de Monaco. The big globular flowers are pale pink which varies little whether they are young or old. Of medium vigour, it branches well and the flowers have good scent.

My Choice. The buds of this fine rose are gold shaded with crimson and they open to pink with a buff reverse. Vigorous in growth, it is well worth having for its scent alone.

Percy Thrower. I can recommend this rose as an excellent variety for the garden and cutting. The flowers are a delightful rose-pink shade and are carried freely.

Perfecta. Superb in shape and size, the flowers are edged with rose paling to ivory and are best in autumn. On light soils, the petals 'burn' badly at the edges. Growth is rather too erect to cover the ground well.

Silver Lining. A rose whose colour is not difficult to blend with others, the flowers being soft rose paling to almost white at the base. The blooms are large, almost always of perfect shape, and the scent is exceptionally good.

Stella. A fine rose, cherry red on the outside petals and pinkish-cream or ivory in the centre. The flowers are long and shapely and plants are of good habit.

Carmine

Eden Rose. One of the most popular rose-pink hybrid teas, the deepest coloured petals matching the lightest coloured of Wendy Cussons. The blooms are magnificent but are not produced too plentifully. Strongly scented.

Rose Gaujard. Although the magenta colour with white reverse of this rose does not appeal to everyone, it is an excellent variety for garden display. The blooms have scent and stand up well to wet weather.

Wendy Cussons. A rose with beautifully shaped flowers although the rather hard cerise colour makes it a poor mixer and it is best planted well separated from reds and yellows. It has a good branching habit with glossy foliage and has won the Royal National Rose Society's Clay Cup for scent.

Red

Christian Dior. This is a fine scarlet rose with beautifully shaped flowers but it is rather prone to mildew and is well above average in height. The young foliage is an attractive coppery colour.

Ena Harkness. One of the best and most popular red roses. The flowers have a tendency to hang their heads.

Fragrant Cloud. This splendid rose has flowers of coral-red colouring, large in size and with outstanding fragrance, as the name implies. It makes a medium-sized bush.

A bed of the hybrid tea rose Ballet, which has large shapely flowers of bluey-pink colouring. Roses of medium height, like Ballet, are particularly well suited to this type of 'block' planting, which is very effective in more spacious gardens

Papa Meilland. An extremely attractive rich red colour, blooms of good shape and a rich scent are attributes which have brought this variety to the fore. It is of medium height.

Uncle Walter. A variety with very large red flowers of classical hybrid tea shape with little tendency to blueing. Growth is extremely vigorous.

Westminster. A brilliant bicolor rose, vivid deep cherry red with yellow reverse. Growth is tall and very vigorous. Strongly scented.

Yellow to Orange
Beauté. A pleasing apricot-yellow with well-formed flowers which stand up well to wet weather. The leathery foliage resists disease.

Gold Crown. A tall grower, upright in habit. The colour of the well-formed blooms is a clear, deep yellow but turns paler with age. It has dark disease-resistant foliage.

King's Ransom. A shapely, medium-sized yellow. It bears its flowers freely and is good for bedding. About medium size.

Lady Belper. An excellent garden rose with beautifully formed blooms of apricot warming to near orange at the heart. It flowers well and has spreading growth of medium height.

Peace. One of the finest roses ever produced. The large flowers vary from pale to deep yellow with variable cerise-pink shading at the edges of the petals. It is very vigorous and needs plenty of space.

Piccadilly. An orange-scarlet and yellow bicolor which pales with age to pink and soft gold. The foliage, reddish when young, changes to dark green with age. It grows about 3 ft. tall.

Spek's Yellow. One of the best bright yellow hybrid teas with medium-sized flowers of good form. Growth is vigorous and the habit very upright. It has dark shiny foliage that resists disease.

Flame and Vermilion

Mischief. The medium-sized flowers are deep pink with orange on the outside of the petals. The coppery coloured foliage, resistant to disease, is good and bushes cover the ground well.

Mrs Sam McGredy. An old rose still outstanding for its bright coppery-orange and red flowers and reddish-bronze foliage. The blooms are produced plentifully and they stand up to wet weather well.

Super Star. Although this is an outstanding rose, the unusual light vermilion colour of the blooms makes it difficult to associate with other colours. The medium-sized blooms are well formed.

Blue

Blue Moon. This well-scented lilac-blue rose is the best choice, perhaps, for those wanting the nearest approach yet to a truly blue rose. Of medium height, it has a branching habit and is slightly stronger, it seems, than Sterling Silver (see below).

Sterling Silver. This lavender-lilac variety has been a flower arranger's favourite since it was introduced in the late 1950s. The flowers have good shape and fragrance and, carefully placed, it is a useful garden rose.

White

Frau Karl Druschki. We still lack a really good white hybrid tea and I still plant this old and very vigorous variety even though its large dead-white flowers do produce traces of pink on the outside.

FLORIBUNDA ROSES

Pink

Chanelle. The buds are a warm amber outside, opening to China pink and cream, but the flowers tend to become wishy-washy with age. It is a vigorous variety that covers the ground well and seldom suffers from disease.

Dearest. A gold medal rose with very pretty pink flowers. The buds are shapely but open to flattish flowers with golden centres; the blooms are carried in large trusses but they do not like wet weather.

Pink Parfait. The pale pink and orange flowers are produced very freely on compact vigorous bushes. The colour is pleasing but may be too delicate for some people. Fragrance is not one of its strong points.

Queen Elizabeth. The soft pink flowers of this fine and very popular floribunda rose are almost of hybrid tea quality but they are produced on very tall bushes.

Vera Dalton. A variety that does well in my own garden; it could be described as a shorter version of Queen Elizabeth. The flowers are a lovely deep pink, bluer in shade than Dearest and more pointed in bud, although they open cup-shaped. Compact in growth, the foliage of this variety is dark green and disease resistant.

Violet Carson. Shrimp pink with a paler reverse and fading a little with age, this is a promising new pink floribunda. The long, pointed flowers are of hybrid tea shape and they are said to stand up to wet weather well. The reddish-bronze foliage enhances the flowers.

Carmine

Daily Sketch. A carmine-pink and silver bicolor, very like Ideal Home, but starting to flower a little earlier. The flowers are large and effective. Medium in height, growth is bushy and covers the ground well.

Paddy McGredy. Described as a hybrid-tea-type floribunda it is certainly very easy to mistake the flowers for those of a hybrid

Left : Lavender Lassie, a handsome lilac-pink floribunda rose with rosette-shaped blooms. This is a tall-growing variety. Right : Rosemary Rose, another delightful floribunda variety with carmine-crimson blooms of rosette shape. This free-flowering variety has bronze-red foliage

tea rose, although it has the free flowering of a floribunda. The cerise colour is not to everyone's liking, but the flowers are scented and produced on bushy plants of medium height.

Rosemary Rose. A charming variety with rosette-shaped flowers resembling those of a double camellia. The colour is carmine-crimson and the bronze-red foliage is also handsome. Growth is vigorous and the

Masquerade, a floribunda rose whose flowers change from deep yellow to pink and deep red. A bold planting of this variety is an arresting sight but, of course, it is not every gardener who finds it attractive

flowers are produced freely throughout the season. Unfortunately the foliage is prone to mildew.

Red

Europeana. A deep crimson floribunda with fully double flowers very freely produced.

Evelyn Fison. The colour is a little lighter than the crimson-scarlet Lilli Marlene, almost a geranium red. The effect is very good and the slight frilling of the petals is pleasing. The foliage is a clean dark green and the growth covers the ground well.

Lilli Marlene. First-rate in every way, this floribunda has velvety crimson-scarlet flowers, fully double and carried in close clusters. Growth is compact and bushy covering the ground well.

Meteor. A variety of dwarf, bushy habit. The semi-double flowers are a bright vermilion and they are produced in good trusses but there is little scent.

Strawberry Fair. The strawberry-red, semi-double flowers of this new variety do not fade as they mature. It flowers freely and is of medium height.

Yellow to Orange

Allgold. Outstanding for its golden-yellow colour which does not fade in the sun or rain. It grows only 2 ft. tall and is resistant to black spot and mildew.

Chinatown. This variety is exceptionally vigorous, growing at least 5 ft. tall in good soil. The large double blooms of hybrid tea shape, produced in small clusters, are a rich yellow. It has healthy glossy foliage and there is some scent.

Elizabeth of Glamis. This fine orange-salmon variety won the Royal National Rose Society's President's International Trophy for the best new rose of the year in 1963 and the Clay Cup for the best new scented rose of the year—this last a most unusual achievement for a floribunda. Also a gold medal winner. Of medium height.

Jiminy Cricket. The colour of this charming rose varies between salmon and pink. It always makes a good show, even in wet weather, and has pleasing reddish foliage.

Woburn Abbey. This is a very showy rose with deep orange flowers of good size. It has fragrance.

Yellow and Carmine

Masquerade. A popular rose although not to everyone's liking. It is interesting from the colour point of view because the flowers change from deep yellow to pink and then deep red. Growth is vigorous and the foliage is disease resistant.

Paintbox. Similar in many ways to Masquerade and many people feel that it is better. The colouring is red and yellow gradually turning to deep red—at first glance one could imagine that two varieties had got mixed together.

Flame and Vermilion

Anna Wheatcroft. The large single flowers are of a reddish-salmon colour which fades a little with age. The yellow stamens show prominently and liven the effect. Of medium height, growth is bushy and the foliage is dark and healthy.

Firecracker. This rose is unique because of the contrast of its bright cherry red colour with yellow centre and golden anthers. It is immensely free flowering and a deservedly popular rose.

Highlight. A good orange-scarlet floribunda with flowers in large trusses. It grows vigorously and resists disease. The old petals are inclined to hang on the trusses when the flowers wither creating an untidy effect.

Korona. This striking flame-scarlet variety with large semi-double blooms is a splendid rose for colourful display. Strong growing.

Orangeade. A popular variety because of its deep orange flowers but I find that they age to an unattractive puce. Growth tends to be a little thin.

Orange Sensation. This is such a hot orange-red that it is difficult to blend with other colours, although it should be happy with a white floribunda such as Iceberg. The flowers are double and produced in large clusters on vigorous, well-branched plants.

Lavender Shades
Lavender Lassie. The lilac-pink, rosette-shaped flowers of this tall-growing rose are very handsome and have good fragrance.

Lavender Pinocchio. The blooms of this variety are greyish-lavender in colour and have pleasant fragrance. It flowers freely.

Magenta. This strong-growing rose has rosy-magenta flowers which it bears freely over an extended period. It also has good fragrance.

White
Iceberg. The best white floribunda for garden display. Growth is rather tall but covers the ground well.

ROSES FOR WALLS AND HEDGES

Roses for walls and hedges are discussed on pp. 66 and 67 and p. 74 respectively.

Two first-rate hybrid tea roses which combine outstanding fragrance with other attributes are Fragrant Cloud (left) and Wendy Cussons. The large blooms of Fragrant Cloud are of coral-red colouring, while those of Wendy Cussons are cerise and not too easy to mix with other colours

CHAPTER ELEVEN

Bulbs, Corms and Tubers
for Colour

I FIND bulbous plants of all kinds a fascinating section of the plant kingdom. There is so much variety and they provide such opportunities for attractive display, formal and informal and in gardens large or small. Tulips and hyacinths are most effective for formal beds and a host of other plants, like daffodils and crocuses, are superb for informal planting, which I must admit is the kind I prefer.

I have said elsewhere in this book (p. 15) that I do not find tulips easy to place as they are too stiff and formal for my liking when planted in blocks of colour. I prefer to grow them individually or in small groups of one colour here and there. Mixing colours can be gay, but it brings its problems, for so often the heights of the different varieties vary, with the result that the bed looks uneven. With formal beds planting is usually done in straight lines, but this type of planting should be avoided wherever possible. Bulbs planted in regimented rows like soldiers on parade may look neat and tidy but it can easily be overdone. It is a different matter, of course, if bulbs are being grown for cutting purposes in, say, a part of the vegetable garden.

Plant in Good Time

A point to remember, particularly where dwarf bulbs are concerned, is to plant them in good time—in September or October, and the earlier the better. Such bulbs as dwarf narcissi, crocuses, *Iris reticulata,* muscari and scillas flower in the early spring and must be given time to make good root growth in the autumn to produce the best results in spring. These are all delightful when planted in small groups on the rock garden, or in some sunny corner where their early flowers will get some protection from the worst of the weather.

Late planting also means that the bulbs do not have sufficient time to make normal growth before the flower spike is produced and often the foliage is immature, which may mean that the second season's flowering will be disappointing. Gardeners have always got to look well ahead and must avoid making mistakes which may not become apparent for months, or in some cases years. First-class bulbs planted at the correct time should develop normally and give good results, but bulbs which have been lying about in bags for months at widely varying temperatures, in a dry atmosphere and planted late, may be a different story. Remember also to plant at the correct depth, for shallow planting is not satisfactory and may lead to the bulbs being damaged by frost.

The author tying in shoots on a specimen of Clematis *Ernest Markham*, a popular variety which belongs to the Viticella section. All clematis like a moist but well-drained soil and the lower part of the stem should be shaded from direct sunshine

Pyracantha atalantioides, *like all the other freely berrying, evergreen Firethorns, is an excellent wall shrub, and will grow well when given a northern aspect. This climber will reach a height of 10ft. or so and have much the same width. The popularity of the Firethorns is an indication of their ease of cultivation*

The remarks opposite do not mean that roses cannot be used satisfactorily in a mixed border, whatever the purists may say. The picture above makes this point clearly. Note, though, that the roses are planted in blocks of individual varieties. In the garden of limited size this is an excellent way of

This planting of the hybrid tea variety Peace, one of the finest roses ever introduced to cultivation, shows the effectiveness of planting in blocks of a single variety. There is too much variation in height and habit for roses to be grown in mixture really satisfactorily. If only a dozen roses can be grown

This strongly coloured floribunda rose, Korona, is ideally suited to its setting—another example of how harmonious greens and neutral white (on the house walls) make it possible to exploit the potentialities of rich colours. For colour display floribunda roses are to be preferred to hybrid teas as they flower more freely and for a much longer period

A gay assortment of climbing and bush roses planted in association with peonies make a charming picture. It will be noticed how the red flowers of the climbing roses are given additional impact by their proximity to those of white and cream colouring

This superb planting of floribunda roses is at the Royal National Rose Society's Gardens at Bone Hill, St Albans, Herts, a garden where roses of all types are grown to perfection. Visiting such a garden is the best possible way of comparing the roses in which one is especially interested

COLOUR WITH MINIMUM TROUBLE

Here are some good kinds to provide colour with the minimum of trouble:

Anemone. For brilliant colouring the St. Brigid and de Caen anemones are outstanding, in shades of crimson, dazzling scarlet, purple, blue and pure white. Plant the tubers 2 to 3 in. deep in a moist, but well-drained soil and in a sunny position. In mild coastal districts the corms may be planted at any time of the year to provide a succession of flower over a long period. In mild coastal districts the corms may be late February or March.

The early-flowering tuberous-rooted *Anemone fulgens* is a splendid sight on a rock garden in April and May when it produces its bright scarlet flowers on 12-in. stems.

Bluebell (see Scilla)

Chionodoxa (Glory of the Snow). Admirable for the rock garden or for naturalising. The dainty clusters of blue flowers are produced on 6-in. stems early in the year. Plant in the early autumn 3 in. deep.

Crocus. The well-known, large-flowered crocuses should be planted about 3 in. deep in well-drained soil in September or October. They are most attractive when planted in grass in clumps, or in a sunny position under trees. Once planted they may be left undisturbed for years. A point to watch when growing crocuses (or for that matter daffodils) in grass is that the grass should not be cut until the crocus leaves have died down, which is usually about the end of May. If they are to build up reserves of food which will allow them to flower well in the following year they must be allowed to complete their growth cycle.

In addition to the large-flowered hybrids there are several charming species, such as

C. tomasinianus, with silvery-lilac flowers on slender stems in early spring. Once established this species will seed itself happily and make large colonies.

There are also autumn-flowering species which should be planted in July or early August, such as the bright blue *C. speciosus,* with vivid orange centres, and the rosy-lilac *C. zonatus* (syn. *C. kotschyanus*). These often increase by self-sown seed which takes about three to four years to flower when left undisturbed.

Crown Imperial (see Fritillaria)

Daffodil (see Narcissus)

Fritillaria. The majestic *Fritillaria imperialis,* commonly known as Crown Imperial, with its glossy green foliage and drooping bells of orange, coppery-red or yellow, borne on sturdy stems 3 ft. or more in height in April, is a most imposing plant. The large bulbs should be planted about 6 in. deep in September. They like a rich, deep soil. Choose a spot sheltered from the early morning sun, or the young growth may be damaged by frost. The bulbs and young growth have an unpleasant smell which is more than made up for by the lovely flowers. Check the price before ordering by the dozen, for the bulbs are expensive and not easy to come by.

Galanthus (Snowdrop). The Common Snowdrop, *G. nivalis,* is one of the earliest heralds of spring, its nodding heads of white and green coming as a delightful surprise in late January and February. There are also numerous other species and named varieties listed in good bulb catalogues. Plant the bulbs about 3 in. deep in the early autumn and leave them undisturbed to form charming clumps. When it becomes necessary to lift and divide such clumps it is best done soon after they have finished flowering and

Left : The Crown Imperial, Fritillaria imperialis, *is an imposing bulbous plant. Its flower heads of drooping orange, coppery-red or yellow bells are borne in April on 3-ft. stems. Right : The Spring Snowflake,* Leucojum vernum, *is a delightful plant with large white flowers tipped with green*

while the foliage is still green, replanting immediately.

Galtonia candicans (Summer Hyacinth). *G. candicans* produces fragrant, white pendulous flowers in August and September on stems 3 to 4 ft. in height. The large bulbs should be planted in a sunny position about 6 in. deep and left undisturbed for several years. October or March are the best months for planting. The plant is still listed as *Hyacinthus candicans* in some catalogues.

Gladiolus. There is now a great variety of gladioli to suit all tastes—large-flowered, dainty Butterfly types and many intermediate hybrids. The corms may be planted from mid-March until late April in well-drained soil and in a sunny position. Where the soil is heavy sprinkle a little sharp sand in the holes before planting the corms about 4 in. deep. This sand, immediately beneath the corms, will improve the drainage and at the same time encourage root action. A little bonemeal will also prove beneficial. The corms are lifted in September or early October and after drying and cleaning are stored in a frost-free place for the winter.

Glory of the Snow (see Chionodoxa)

Grape Hyacinth (see Muscari)

Hyacinth (see Hyacinthus)

Hyacinthus (Hyacinth). Fragrant hyacinths are delightful for window boxes or tubs, as well as for formal bedding schemes. Plant the bulbs in September, October or November about 3 to 4 in. deep and about 6 to 8 in. apart. In a sunny position beneath a window the colourful heads will be most welcome in the early spring. The blue *Hyacinthus amethystinus* with 6-in. stems is most decorative on the rock garden in May.

Iris. The bulbous irises are quite distinct from the 'flag' or tall bearded irises which have perennial rootstocks. The first to flower are the dwarf species, such as *I. danfordiae* with deep lemon-yellow flowers on 3-in. stems in January and February, and *I. reticulata* which bears its blue flowers in February and March. The Dutch, Spanish and English irises, which flower in that order, begin about the first week in June and continue in the case of the English varieties into July. They are grown in many gardens for cut flowers.

The Dutch and Spanish varieties should be planted about 3 in. deep in the autumn. Plant the English irises about an inch deeper. In severe weather a top dressing of peat or bracken will form a useful protection. All these irises like a sunny position and a well-drained soil with plenty of moisture during the growing season. They have stems about 2 ft. in height. Plant *danfordiae* and *reticulata* in August-September 4 in. deep.

Leucojum (Snowflake). The snowflakes are taller and much larger than the snowdrops which they resemble somewhat. The first to flower in February and March is *L. vernum*, the Spring Snowflake, bearing large white bells tipped with green on 6-in. stems. This is a delightful plant for naturalising in groups. It is followed early in May by *L. aestivum*, the Summer Snowflake, which produces several flowers of a similar colour on stems about $1\frac{1}{2}$ ft. high. The bulbs of these two species should be planted in September or October, about 3 in. deep. The little Autumn Snowflake, *L. autumnale*, should be planted in July or early August in a well-drained, sandy loam. In late September it produces nodding, white, pink-flushed flowers on slender 6-in. stems. It is a charming but not spectacular plant. The snowflakes should be left undisturbed once they have been planted.

Lilium. The elegant genus *Lilium* com-

Left : The easily grown, shapely Regal Lily, Lilium regale, has white flowers flushed gold on the outside and purplish without. Right : The tigridias, Tiger Flowers, provide gay splashes of colour in late summer with their spotted blooms of scarlet, bronze, orange and yellow

prises a great company of species and hybrids. They vary greatly in colour, height and habit, and, generally speaking, they are best planted in October or November, except on heavy soils where spring planting may be advisable. There are, however, exceptions, for the fragrant white Madonna lily, *L. candidum,* should be planted soon after it has finished flowering in July. Late August or September is the best period to move bulbs of this lily, which should be covered with only about an inch of soil.

Stem-rooting lilies should be planted 8 to 9 in. deep (the easily grown white, flushed gold Regal Lily, *L. regale*; the orange Tiger Lily, *L. tigrinum*; the choice white, gold and red spotted *L. auratum* and the white, crimson spotted *L. speciosum* are some which fall in this category). The depth of planting will, of course, be governed by the type of soil in the garden, and in some cases the bulbs may have to be planted only about 4 in. deep, top-dressing later with leafsoil. As a general rule for other lilies 5 to 6 in. is a satisfactory planting depth.

Montbretia. The montbretias are now botanically known as *Crocosmia,* but that does not make any difference to their cultivation, which is simple. The corms should be planted in March or April about 3 in. deep in well-drained soil and in a sunny position. They increase rapidly, so should be planted at least 6 in. apart. The slender, sword-like leaves are arranged like a fan and the graceful flower spikes in shades of orange, yellow and crimson appear in August and September. In exposed gardens the corms should be protected in severe weather with a layer of peat, bracken or straw.

Muscari (Grape Hyacinth). Flowering in early spring, the deep blue muscari are admirable for planting in little groups on the rock garden or for massing in the front of a border. Plant the bulbs in early autumn about 3 in. deep and about 3 or 4 in. apart. There is also a white form, and a plume-like variety, *M. comosum monstrosum,* which bears mauve, twisted flowers in May, some weeks later than most muscari appear.

Narcissus (Daffodil). The narcissi range from the tiny varieties suitable for the rock garden, naturalising in grass or for growing in pans in a cold greenhouse, to the elegant and colourful hybrids which breeders in this country, and particularly in Ireland, have produced in ever-increasing numbers during the past thirty years or so. As far as the little narcissi are concerned these are best planted 2 to 3 in. deep in August, but the trumpet daffodils, the large-cupped varieties and the many other large forms should be planted in September or October. Plant these with about 6 in. of soil over the noses of the bulbs, or 4 to 5 in. where the soil is heavy. Daffodils planted informally in groups under trees or in grassland are seen at their best. Bulb catalogues list varieties in a diversity of colours and forms sufficient to suit all tastes and pockets.

Ranunculus. The Turban or Persian Buttercup ranunculus make a gorgeous display in many brilliant colours in a sunny border in May and early June. Plant the tubers with the 'claws' downwards about 2 to 3 in. deep in well-drained soil in February or March. They like plenty of moisture during the growing season and the tubers should be lifted in July and stored in dry sand.

Snowdrop (see Galanthus)

Scilla. The Bluebells are listed in bulb catalogues under *Scilla,* to which genus they used to belong but have been moved to the genus *Endymion* by the botanists. The common bluebell and the various pink and white forms are delightful when planted in a wild or woodland garden. Plant in the autumn 2 to 4 in. deep. The smaller Siberian Squill, *Scilla sibirica,* is well suited for pockets on the rock garden where its dainty bright blue flowers on 4-in. stems are a picture in March and April. Plant the bulbs about 3 in. deep. This squill associates well with little clumps of dwarf narcissi.

Siberian Squill (see Scilla)

Snowdrop (see Galanthus)

Snowflake (see Leucojum)

Summer Hyacinth (see Galtonia)

Tiger Flower (see Tigridia)

Tigridia (Tiger Flower). The brilliant Mexican Tiger Flowers (forms of *Tigridia pavonia*) are outstanding from July onwards when planted in full sun in well-drained soil, preferably in a sheltered corner of the garden. Plant about 3 in. deep in April or early May, lift in October and store in dry sand away from frost for the winter. The flowers, borne on 18 in. stems are about 4 in. across and are available in shades of glowing scarlet, bronze, orange and yellow with red-spotted centres and other variations. The flowers last only for a few hours but more appear each sunny day.

Tulip (see Tulipa)

Tulipa (Tulip). Probably more tulips are planted than any other kind of bulb, with the exception of narcissi. The Early Single and Early Double tulips start to flower in April, followed in late April by the long-stemmed Mendel varieties. In the month of May there is a galaxy of Triumph, Darwin, Parrot, Rembrandt, Cottage, and Lily-flowered tulips, among other glorious types. By carefully selecting one's varieties these tulips will give a brilliant display of colour for weeks on end.

In addition to these bedding tulips, there are the early-flowering tulips suitable for the rock garden, such as the striking *kaufmanniana, fosteriana* and *greigii* hybrids with exquisitely beautiful flowers. These flowers are borne on stems 6 to 8 in., 1 to $1\frac{1}{2}$ ft. and 9 to 12 in. tall respectively. Among the many species is the dwarf *T. praestans* from Central Asia which brings forth glossy vermilion-scarlet blooms in early April, as many as four on a branching stem. This species often causes considerable comment.

Several species produce more than one flower on a stem, and when modern hybrids do likewise it gives some indication of a cross made years ago by the plant breeders. It is not sensational and is unlikely to mean a fortune around the corner.

Plant tulip bulbs in October and November with about 4 in. of soil above the nose of the bulb. The smaller bulbs of the rock-garden varieties may be planted a little less deep.

CHAPTER TWELVE

Rock Garden Plants
for Colour

THE term 'rock-garden plant' covers a great many plants used to provide colour and interest in rock gardens, dry walls and sink gardens. These plants are also called alpines, another term not readily defined, but as a general rule one must be careful not to use on the rock garden those plants which grow too large or are liable to become invasive. He is a clever gardener, however, who always places his rock plants in the right place, whether from the viewpoint of size or colour, but mistakes in planting provide useful experience. In any case I believe that the gay clash of, say, violet aubrieta and yellow alyssum is acceptable for a brief period after the drabness of winter. Always aim to have the colours well mixed and the interest spread over as long a period as can be arranged.

The rock-garden specialist frowns on the use of annual and biennial plants and would not dream of using gazanias, mesembryanthemums, dwarf antirrhinums and other summer-flowering plants to fill gaps, but if such plants give us pleasure in our own gardens let us enjoy them.

SITE AND PREPARATION

A rock garden should be in an open, sunny position away from overhanging trees. Ideally a south- or south-west-facing slope with thoroughly well-drained soil is desirable, for while rock plants like plenty of moisture during the growing season, many of them detest winter wet. In their mountain homes they are for months protected by a deep, crisp layer of snow which keeps the plants dry and at an even, if low, temperature. Obviously we cannot provide such winter conditions, but we can do our best to provide good drainage. If we have unusual and favourite plants these can be given protection from excessive winter rains by using small cloches, or just a sheet of glass supported over the plant by a piece of stout wire. The keen gardener will adopt ingenious methods to protect his treasures.

CONSTRUCTION

Where suitable stone is available locally it is far better and more economical to make use of it, rather than, for instance, transporting limestone from the Lake District to a Sussex garden, where the local warm-looking sandstone would be much more in keeping with the surroundings. Large flints or lumps of broken concrete are sometimes used for reasons of economy, but they do not weather readily and it is best to avoid them whenever possible.

If the rock garden is on a level site and the soil is heavy, it will be wise to make some provision for drainage before starting to place any stone. If a deep hole is dug and filled with coarse rubble this will drain away surplus moisture, and a layer of coarse ash or shingle just above and around the top of the soakaway will improve the drainage over the whole area of the rock garden. Where the rock garden is on a natural slope there should be no need for such work. Wherever the site is, it should be dug over and all perennial weeds carefully removed, otherwise they may become established beneath the rocks and can be extremely troublesome.

When placing the stones try and form natural-looking strata, and avoid placing pieces of rock on end—they will look like almonds decorating a cake. Ample sifted soil will be required to use around the pieces of rock, and the soil must be rammed firmly behind and around each piece.

Planting

When the construction work is completed do not start planting immediately, but wait for a week or two for the soil to get settled. It is best for the amateur to begin with a collection of plants that are easily grown and to make a selection which will provide colour and interest over as long a period as possible. (The general advice given on the use of colour in Chapter One should prove helpful at this time.) Later, when these have become established, try a few of the more difficult alpines which may be particularly interesting to you.

Rock plants are grown in pots by nurserymen and should be planted firmly. For this reason it is wise to let the soil settle on a newly-made rock garden before planting. If the ball of soil is very full of roots, press the soil gently and loosen the roots at the bottom, removing the 'crocks'

if there are any among the roots at the bottom. With a trowel make a hole deep enough to take the roots without having to bunch them up, then gently but firmly fill in around the ball with fresh soil, leaving the neck of the plant level with the surface soil.

Propagation

Alpine plants can be increased by sowing seed or by taking cuttings. Named varieties of aubrieta, helianthemum and the like will not come true to colour from seed, and must be increased by cuttings. These are made from young, non-flowering shoots, up to about 2 in. long. Remove the lower leaves and with a sharp knife or razor blade make a cut immediately beneath a leaf joint. Insert the cuttings into pots, pans or a propagating frame containing moist sharp silver sand or a very sandy loam. Water them in and then stand them in a shaded frame and spray them overhead with water occasionally, using a fine syringe. These cuttings do not require heat and can be taken in the early spring, or later in the year soon after the plants have been trimmed back after flowering.

February is a good month to sow alpine seeds, although if you have saved seed from your own primulas this should be sown as soon as it is ripe during the summer, and it will germinate quickly in cool, moist conditions. Seeds of alpines should be sown in pans or boxes containing a gritty, well-drained compost and these only require the lightest covering with sifted soil. Water carefully with a can fitted with a fine rose, then cover the pans or boxes with sheets of asbestos, or glass and brown paper, to exclude the light, and stand in a cold frame or cold greenhouse to germinate.

Some alpine plants lend themselves to division—armeria, sedum, sempervivum,

Left: The Mountain Avens, Dryas octopetala, *an attractive plant with creamy-white flowers. Centre:* Erythronium dens-canis, *with distinctive flowers and marbled foliage. Right: The choice, bright blue, autumn-flowering* Gentiana sino-ornata

some campanulas and dianthus, for instance. This can be done carefully in the spring or autumn and the small pieces which are removed with a little root should be potted singly. They should be kept in a cool, shaded frame for a week or two until they are established.

CHOICE OF PLANTS

If your soil is naturally alkaline, that is it contains lime or is chalky, there are certain plants to avoid, unless separate pockets of lime-free soil are made on the rock garden. This, however, is not always satisfactory, owing to water containing lime seeping through and contaminating the soil. Plants which do not tolerate lime include rhododendrons (some of the dwarf species are charming for the rock garden), hardy heathers (other than the winter-flowering *Erica carnea* and its varieties), lithospermums, the bright blue, autumn-flowering *Gentiana sino-ornata* and its hybrids, and lewisias, which in any case are not plants for the beginner, and do best in or on top of a dry wall.

A good alpine nursery would be happy to supply a collection of, say, 50 different varieties of rock plants suitable for the beginner. Depending on the size of the rock garden you could have two or three plants of each variety and plant the varieties in groups. This will prove more effective than single plants dotted around. Such a collection should include armerias, named varieties of aubrieta, campanulas, dianthus, the creamy-white-flowered Mountain Avens (*Dryas octopetala*), geranium species, helianthemums (Sun Roses), *Phlox subulata* and its hybrids, potentillas, saxifrages, sedums, sempervivums (House Leeks), fragrant thymes, and various veronicas.

PLANTS FOR SPECIAL PURPOSES

Shade

A shady rock garden can be a problem but the following plants will do quite well; *Anemone nemorosa* and its varieties, the delightful little creeping dogwood, *Cornus canadensis,* with white, petal-like bracts, hardy cyclamen, *Daphne blagayana* with creamy-white fragrant flowers, the purplish-rose Dog's Tooth Violet (*Erythronium dens-canis*), the blue *Mertensia virginica* and *Omphalodes verna,* pulmonarias

Lilies, such as the Madonna Lily (Lilium candidum) shown above, combine admirably with other flowers of similar stature to create a charming picture. The rigidity of the lilies and delphiniums is counteracted by the soft, flowing lines of the rambler roses. This planting scheme has a natural affinity with the picturesque cottage

What could be more beautiful than naturalised daffodils in such a setting! There is only one thing which can cause a problem with this type of planting: the grass should not be cut until the top growth has died down naturally, which means about late May or early June. If the planting is near the house some gardeners might find this a little untidy

Part of Percy Thrower's
garden below the water
pool. Moisture-loving
mulas, alpine dianthus, vi
and hostas are plants provic
a display in early summ
With careful planning a
garden can provide colou
one form or another for m
of the year

The restrained and varied
colour of the plants in this
rock garden may have less
immediate impact than, say,
the gay clash of violet aubrieta
and yellow alyssum, but the
effect is more lasting and in a
quieter way more satisfying

in variety, the lilac-blue *Ramonda myconi* and the pink *Saxifraga umbrosa* (London Pride) and its varieties.

Poor Soil

Where the soil is poor and plants are required that need little attention, a selection of the following should provide the answer: acaenas, ajugas, armerias (Thrift), epimediums, erinus, the golden-yellow *Euphorbia myrsinites*, festuca (ornamental grasses), helianthemums in colours from yellow and orange shades to deep red, the red *Polygonum vaccinifolium,* the apricot and crimson blotched *Potentilla tonguei,* the pink *Saponaria ocymoides,* sedums (Stonecrops) and sempervivums in variety, *Thymus serpyllum* and its varieties in shades of pink, mauve and white, *Veronica filiformis,* blue, and vinca (Periwinkle).

Chalk Soils

Where the soil in a garden is lime or chalk the following plants will thrive: achilleas, aethionemas, alyssum, anemones, armerias, campanulas, dianthus, *Dryas octopetala, Erinus alpinus,* erodium, hardy geranium species, *Gypsophila repens,* helianthemums, hypericum, iberis, *Leontopodium alpinum* (Edelweiss), linum (Flax), oenothera, *Phlox subulata* and its varieties, saxifrages, scabiosa, sempervivums, and thymes.

Plants With Decorative Foliage

We must not forget the useful range of plants that have decorative foliage when other plants have finished flowering, namely *Achillea tomentosa, Artemisia lanata, Dryas octopetala,* epimediums, *Helichrysum marginatum, Sedum spathulifolium,* sempervivums, those colourful dwarf shrubs *Berberis stenophylla semperflorens* and *B. thunbergii atropurpurea nana,* and the many and varied dwarf conifers.

BULBS AND CORMS FOR THE ROCK GARDEN

Bulbs are, of course, a delight not only in the spring but almost throughout the year if planted from the following selection: allium (decorative members of the onion family), chionodoxa, crocus (winter, spring and autumn flowering), galanthus (Snowdrop), *Iris reticulata* and other dwarf species, leucojum (Snowflake), for spring and autumn, muscari (Grape Hyacinth), dwarf narcisse, puschkinia, scilla (Squill), dwarf tulips, and for a warm, sunny corner, the Zephyr Flower, zephyranthes.

Then there are various hardy cyclamen which flower in spring, summer or autumn, namely the carmine-flowered *C. coum,* the rosy-pink *C. neapolitanum* and the crimson *C. repandum,* among others. In addition, some such as *neapolitanum, europaeum* and *repandum* have most attractive mottled leaves which are still a delight in the depth of winter. Cyclamen corms should be planted in partial shade in a gritty, moist soil with plenty of leafmould and preferably some lime. Once they are planted they should be left undisturbed to seed themselves and form a colony. The corms should be pressed into the ground so that the top of the corm is only just covered with soil.

SINK GARDENS

Where space is restricted alpine plants may be grown in old stone sinks or troughs and can be a charming feature on a roof or patio garden, providing colour and interest out of all proportion to their size. And, of course, in more spacious surroundings too they can add much to the overall picture, if carefully sited and planted.

Such sinks must have a drainage hole with a layer of crocks or shingle on the bottom. Cover this drainage material with

A well-planted sink garden can be made to represent a mountain landscape in miniature. The way to success lies in a careful choice of rock plants, including trailing kinds to drape over the edges, and, perhaps, a dwarf conifer or so to simulate trees

a layer of leaves or rough peat and then fill to within about an inch of the top of the sink with a well-drained gritty compost. The soil may or may not have to be lime-free, depending on what plants are to be grown. The sink should be at least 6 in. deep. The larger and deeper the better, for a sizable trough will not dry out so quickly in hot weather. It should be stood in an open, sunny position and if it is possible to stand it on a stone pillar or balustrade at about eye level it will be more easily admired.

A few pieces of stone—tufa is very suitable—can be used but do not overdo the stone or there will be little room for plants. This rock garden in miniature should have a sprinkling of stone chippings scattered around the plants as a finishing touch. This will not only assist drainage around the collar of the plants but will also deter weeds. Be careful not to use limestone chippings if the plants are intolerant of lime. Do not use rampant plants such as many of the sedums and the stronger growing House

Leeks, and remember that miniature roses do not as a rule live long when planted in sinks. Plants that do thrive are the rose-red *Aethionema* Warley Rose, the rose-pink *Androsace sarmentosa* (to trail over the edge), the white to pink *Armeria caespitosa,* the blue *Campanula cochlearifolia* (syn. *C. pusilla*), the rose-red *Dianthus alpinus* (which likes lime), *D. neglectus* (which does not like lime) of similar colouring, the violet-purple *Erinus alpinus,* the yellow *Iris pumila,* the golden-yellow *Morisia monantha, Phlox douglasii* and its varieties in various colours, Kabschia varieties of saxifrage, and the small, compact *Sempervivum arachnoideum.* The little Noah's Ark Juniper, *Juniperus communis compressa,* is a very slow-growing conifer which is admirably suited for a miniature rock garden.

Once planted a sink garden requires little attention other than hand weeding occasionally and watering in dry weather. Where the sink is large enough a few small bulbs, such as miniature narcissi and the smallest crocuses, may also be planted.

CHAPTER THIRTEEN

Dry Wall Plants for Colour

A DRY wall in a garden can be made a colourful feature by planting suitable rock plants between the horizontally laid stones. A dry retaining wall is one that is constructed without the use of cement, and rectangular pieces of sandstone are often used for this purpose. The warm golden colour of this stone makes a pleasing background for rock plants, and is not so hard or cold-looking as granite which is extensively used for walling, instead of hedges, in northern counties. Nevertheless granite is most durable and is rarely damaged by frost, so if this stone is available locally use it by all means. It will look more in keeping than transported stone of an entirely different nature. It is, however, more difficult to lay being usually of odd, boulder-like form, rather than rectangular.

A retaining wall has soil behind it, that is, it is built to support soil on a sloping site, and between each layer of horizontal stones is placed about an inch or so of soil, instead of mortar, in which plants will grow happily. Ideally the planting should be done as the wall is built, but in practice this seldom seems to happen. There is, of course, a limit to the height of a wall which is not bound together with mortar, and the higher the wall the broader must be the base. The face of the wall should be gently

inclined, not vertical. This slight angle will keep the soil moist between the horizontal stones, and, with a row of large pieces among the top, sloping inwards, rain water will get to the plants' roots in the soil behind the walling.

An attractive feature can be made by constructing a rectangular island site with a surrounding retaining wall, say 2 ft. in height, and filling this with soil. This will then provide not only a sunny side, but also a shaded side suitable for those alpines that will not flourish in hot sun. The top of the island can be planted as a scree for rock plants that like sun and good drainage, as well as small bulbs—dwarf narcissi, crocuses, miniature irises, scillas and tulip species—and a selection of dwarf conifers, which are so charming throughout the year.

Whatever type of garden wall is constructed, even a wall made of peat blocks (which can be a charming feature for peat-loving plants), it is important to make sure that the foundation is properly prepared. One should start by taking out a shallow trench into which is put a layer of old ashes, pebbles or similar material to provide drainage. Over this layer put inverted turves or coarse peat and then start the first row of stones, which should be large and about 3 in. below the surface soil. This

A gay planting of spring flowers on a dry wall at Quarry Park, Shrewsbury. Dry walls exposed to plenty of sunshine provide the gardener with an opportunity to grow many colourful plants and, as explained below, shady walls can also be clothed effectively

will give a firm base upon which to build the wall.

SUITABLE PLANTS

Sunny Walls

A sunny dry wall can be a very warm spot so choose plants that enjoy such conditions. Some of these are, of course, suitable for the rock garden also, and have been mentioned in that chapter. Such plants are the rose-coloured *Acantholimon glumaceum,* the summer-flowering *Aethionema* Warley Rose with many heads of rose-pink flowers on sturdy little stems, the various alyssums and arabis, the long-flowering, pink androsaces with attractive rosettes of grey, hairy leaves, aubrietas, in shades of mauve, lavender, pink and deep red, and campanulas and dianthus in variety. Sun roses (helianthemums) flower throughout the summer and present no difficulty. If they are trimmed back as soon as the flowers start to fade a second crop will often be produced. Clipping also keeps the plants bushy. There are many different named varieties in shades of orange, copper, yellow, glowing red and pink. An old favourite of mine is *H. rhodanthe carneum,* with clear pink flowers and ash-grey little leaves.

Another easy plant is the Mountain Avens, *Dryas octopetala,* which forms a close dark green mat of attractive leaves and bears large white flowers with prominent gold centres in early summer. It will grow in the poorest soil and likes full sun. Other colourful plants are *Lithospermum* Heavenly Blue; *Phlox subulata* in variety; *Iberis sempervirens* (perennial candytuft which has several named varieties); lewisias; *Polygonum vaccinifolium* with erect spikes of deep pink flowers in late summer and autumn; *Saponaria ocymoides,* a trailing soapwort with bright pink flowers; many kinds of houseleek (semper-

Left : Dwarf brooms like Cytisus kewensis, *with sulphur yellow flowers, are a lovely sight when cascading over a dry stone wall. Right : A well planted rock bank makes an attractive path-side feature when planned with a careful eye for colour harmonies and pleasing contrasts*

vivum) and sedums; forms of *Saxifraga aizoon*, and *Veronica prostrata* in variety. For a really well-drained, sunny corner the Californian fuchsia, *Zauschneria californica*, makes a fine splash of scarlet in the late summer and autumn. The foliage is grey which adds to the attraction.

Shady Walls
Hardy ferns, such as the little *Asplenium trichomanes* with elegant green 6-in. fronds borne on black, shiny stems, are excellent for this purpose. Where it is moist as well as shady the common primrose makes a charming feature and some of the other dwarf primulas can be planted. The little

Hutchinsia alpina forms a close mat of green covered in spring with dainty white flowers. The Navel Wort, *Omphalodes cappadocica,* has erect stems about 9 in. high bearing forget-me-not-like blue flowers during the summer, and the closer-growing ramondas are admirable for a cool, north-facing crevice. The species from the Pyrenees, *Ramonda myconi*, has sprays of lilac-blue flowers, resembling that of the potato but on 3-in. stems. With a selection of these and many other plants, not forgetting small bulbous plants for the top soil of a retaining wall, even quite a small stretch of walling can be a delightful and interesting feature in a garden.

CHAPTER FOURTEEN

Plants for Paved Areas

A PAVED terrace, patio or path is a permanent feature in a garden, and while the initial outlay may seem heavy, there is neither the upkeep nor the mowing that grass requires to be kept in good condition. A terrace or patio, moreover, can be used as a sitting-out area almost immediately

A paved area, such as below, provides the enthusiast with the opportunity to grow many plants between the stones, these forming pleasing colour patterns. Mat-forming chamomile, mint and thyme, dwarf campanulas and dianthus are some of the plants which enjoy such an environment

after rain and it can be made very bright and colourful indeed by planting suitable plants between the stones. Such areas, too, are ideal sites for stone sinks containing alpines (see pp. 99-100) and other containers providing homes for many different plants (see p. 143). Paving is far more satisfactory than grass for a path that is going to have regular use, particularly near the house where grass can become worn in the summer and muddy in the winter.

The rock plant enthusiast will make up his mind that paving offers him opportunities to grow many attractive plants between the intersections of the stones, either in formal rectangular paving or even more so in random or crazy paving. Where planting is done between rectangular paving, it will probably be necessary to chip the corners of the stones to make a space for the plants. A fern trowel is a useful tool to remove some of the soil, ash or sand on which the slabs have been laid, and this is replaced with a little gritty potting compost in which the rock plants will quickly make roots.

Few plants will endure being trodden upon frequently, so do not overdo the planting in the middle of the path but concentrate mainly on the sides. Choose low-growing carpeting plants or those of

Left : A colourful pavement planting of lavender, thyme and variegated ornamental grass (holcus).
Right : Thymes and dianthus clothing a paved area to make a delightful combination of colours

neat, bushy habit. It is not advisable to introduce plants in a path where it happens to run beneath trees, because the plants will not usually flourish, and in addition they may too often become slippery due to drip from overhanging branches.

Nurserymen grow rock plants in pots and this means that they can be planted at almost any time except when the ground is frozen. When planting make the soil firm around the ball of roots, and should the pot-grown plant be root-bound, loosen the soil around the lower roots, removing any crocks that may happen to be in the soil so that the roots will quickly become established in the new soil. Then water the plants with a can fitted with a fine rose, and should the weather be dry water daily until the plants have happily settled in.

Where a path is in the shade on the north side of a house, or beneath overhanging trees, the stone slabs can become dangerously slippery in wet weather. If the stones are brushed over with a solution of domestic bleach this will usually cure the trouble, at any rate for a time, but do not saturate any plants with the solution. It is unlikely, however, that there will be plants growing in a path with such an aspect.

SOME PLANTING SUGGESTIONS

The following plants are suitable for planting between the intersections of paving stones and will make a pathway both interesting and colourful: acaenas, compact varieties of armeria (Thrift), *Achillea prichardii*, the recently introduced *Anthemis nobilis* Treneague, a non-flowering chamomile which forms a dense green mat; and aubrietas, in shades of mauve, lavender, pink and red, and dwarf forms of dianthus, all of which like a well-drained, sunny position.

Then there is the minute white daisy, *Bellium minutum*; *Erigeron mucronatus* with white and pink flowers from spring until autumn; dwarf campanulas, such as C. *cochlearifolia* (syn. *C. pusilla*) with dainty little bright blue bells on 3-in. stems, and the spreading *Dryas octopetala* with dark green leaves and most pleasing large, creamy-white flowers with golden centres which are freely produced in early summer. *D. octopetala* is easily raised from seed, in fact, in some gardens self-sown seedlings appear in gravelly soil.

The grey-green tufty grass, *Festuca crinum-ursi* (syn. *F. eskia*) is decorative and the carpeting *Thymus serpyllum* and its varieties in shades of mauve, pink and white flowers, which are most loved by bees, and the Corsican Mint, *Mentha requienii*, are strongly aromatic prostrate plants. This mint forms a thin veil of light green with tiny mauve flowers.

For a cool corner *Hutchinsia alpina* will form a green mat covered from May onwards with little white flowers, and for quite a different position that is dry and in full sun, there are various houseleeks, or sempervivums. The floriferous alpine phloxes and *Saxifraga aizoon* and its forms are also useful, and *Potentilla tonguei*, which bears rich apricot, crimson blotched flowers on 5-in. stems off and on throughout the summer.

Where there is a wide paved terrace or patio it may be possible to introduce one or two dwarf conifers, such as the erect, always admired Noah's Ark juniper, *Juniperus communis compressa,* but care should be taken not to overdo the planting of these dwarfs. Some are of prostrate habit but are vigorous and will eventually cover quite a considerable area so they must be planted only where there is ample space. If a specimen is placed a few feet back from a broad path or terrace it will make an attractive evergreen carpet and will not then encroach too much over the actual paving.

Sited at the end of a formal terrace or wide-paved path the Golden Irish Yew (*Taxus baccata fastigiata aurea*) will make a striking erect column with an eventual height of about 15 ft. The golden sheen is pleasing throughout the year. If something less formal is desired, perhaps to associate with a nearby bed of hardy heathers, then the dwarf form of the European mountain pine, *Pinus mugo pumilio*, makes a dense spreading rather Japanese-looking little tree about 2 ft. in height. It is very hardy and does not object to lime in the soil.

The ingenious gardener will find many ways of making a path or terrace colourful and interesting, rather than just a stretch of stone to provide a footway from A to B.

CHAPTER FIFTEEN

Chrysanthemums for Display

WITH the exception of the rose, few plants have been developed more extensively or over so long a period as the chrysanthemum. As a result it is a wonderfully varied flower with all kinds of forms and colours, and a flowering season which, even without the aid of artificially controlled day length, extends from July to January. The later varieties require the protection of a greenhouse to preserve their flowers from injury by frost, but this still leaves a period of three or four months during which chrysanthemums can play a very important part in the open garden.

For this purpose they possess a quality that is often overlooked, the ability to withstand, far better than most plants, the shock of being transplanted when fully grown. The Pompon and Korean varieties are particularly good in this respect. This means that it is possible to keep chrysanthemums in reserve until they are really needed; to grow them, perhaps, in the vegetable garden or in some other place where they will not need to be decorative, and then to remove them to the display beds just as they are about to come into bloom. This can be a very useful method of filling up gaps caused by the removal of earlier flowering plants.

There is a bewilderingly large number of varieties but a great many of these are not suitable for garden display. They either flower too late, or they have flowers that are readily damaged by rain, or they have been specially bred to produce large flowers for show or for cutting. For the garden it is quantity rather than size of bloom that really matters. The pompon varieties with their tight little flowers can be far more effective than some of the show varieties that will produce only five or six big blooms per plant. Single-flowered and double-flowered chrysanthemums of the so-called Korean type are excellent display plants and they will go on flowering outdoors a good deal later than most. All the same some of the larger flowered varieties can be used if they have good firm petals, and there can be no denying that what they lack in mass display they make up in the individual beauty of their flowers.

PROPAGATION

For whatever purpose chrysanthemums are being grown the method of starting them off is the same. Young shoots are removed from old plants, are prepared as cuttings and are then rooted in a greenhouse or frame. If no such facilities are available it

Chrysanthemum propagation. Left: Sturdy young shoots from which cuttings will be made are removed from the old plants with a sharp knife. Right: Each cutting is prepared by trimming the base just below a leaf joint

is possible to grow chrysanthemums from what are sometimes called Irishman's cuttings, i.e. shoots pulled from old plants with a few roots attached. This method works quite well with many of the free growing Korean and Rubellum varieties, but is not so satisfactory for the more highly developed varieties with large flowers. Ordinary cuttings are taken in February and March. Irishman's cuttings

Left: The lower leaves are removed from the cuttings, taking care when doing this not to damage the stem. Right: The cuttings can be rooted in 3-in. pots of sandy soil in a propagating frame or in a box covered with a sheet of glass and placed in a greenhouse

Left: The rooted cuttings are grown in pots or boxes and are planted outside in late April or early May, after hardening off. Right: Removing the tip of the plant will make it produce several side shoots. The plants are staked immediately after planting

need not be taken until April and can go straight into a bed of well-broken soil in the open. The true cuttings must be prepared as I have already described for other cuttings, and are best rooted in a propagating frame or a box covered with a sheet of glass and placed in the greenhouse. As soon as they are rooted and commence to grow, they must either be planted 2 or 3 in. apart in shallow boxes, or be potted

Left: Feeding with a general fertiliser will encourage the production of good, sturdy growth. Right: Disbudding, or the removal of side buds, is carried out where large blooms are required. This task should be done as soon as the flower buds can be seen

Left : When the plants have finished flowering, those plants needed for the production of material from which cuttings can be made are labelled and lifted

individually in 3 in. or 3½ in. pots. In either case John Innes potting compost or a soilless compost plus fertilisers can be used.

Soon after this the chrysanthemums must be put in an unheated frame where they will remain for two or three weeks to be hardened off before being planted out. This may be in late April or early May.

PLANTING IN THE GARDEN

At this stage there are two possibilities, either to plant where the chrysanthemums are to flower, or to plant in a reserve bed from which they will be removed to the flowering positions when they are required there. In either case the ground must be well dug and fed with a good all-purpose fertiliser scattered over the surface at about 4 oz. per square yard. The plants must have enough room to develop properly, which means that if they are in

rows these should be at least 2 ft. apart with 15 in. between plants in the rows. This is the most convenient method if plants are being grown in a reserve bed, but if they are going directly to their flowering positions it may give a better effect to space them evenly about 18 in. apart.

Stake them immediately so that their stems can be properly tied in from the outset. Chrysanthemum growth is brittle and easily broken by wind. One cane or strong stick per plant will suffice, and it need be no taller than the advertised height of the plants—about 2 ft. for most Korean, Rubellum and Pompon varieties, and 3 ft. for the larger flowered varieties. Then when the supports have been pushed well into the soil and the stems have grown up around them they will be concealed from view.

After planting out, the tip of each plant should be pinched out to make it produce side growths. Subsequently the tips of these can also be removed to make the plants even more bushy.

AFTERCARE

During the following months the plants must be sprayed occasionally to keep them clear of greenfly, capsid bugs and other pests, the soil around them must be hoed to kill weeds, and an occasional feed should be given. BHC and DDT will take care of the pests and any good all-purpose fertiliser can be used as a feed.

Books on chrysanthemum cultivation usually have a lot to say about disbudding and timing. Neither need trouble the gardener who is simply growing for display, unless he wants some large flowers, in which case he will have to do some dis-budding. This means that the natural tendency of the chrysanthemum to produce its flowers in sprays, not all opening at the same time, must be controlled by removing all the side buds or shoots and only leaving one central flower bud on each stem to develop. The time to do this is as soon as the flower buds can be seen, at which stage they will be tight and green and not much bigger than a large pin's head. The surrounding buds, or any shoots appearing lower down the stems, are then rubbed or pinched out or removed with the point of a knife. It is rather a fiddling job which the enthusiastic chrysanthemum grower thoroughly enjoys, for in each tiny bud he can foresee the splendid bloom that is going to materialise. But as I have already said, if you are growing chrysanthemums simply for mass display, it is best to forget all about disbudding.

If the chrysanthemums are grown in a reserve bed a sharp spade should be thrust

These 'stool' plants are then placed in boxes of good soil (as above) or planted in a frame

into the soil in a circle about 9 in. from the base of the plant to sever far-reaching roots. Do this a week before lifting and then, a day before lifting, water the plants thoroughly. Lift and replant with as little delay as possible. It is as well to prepare the holes for the plants before commencing to lift them. Round off the whole operation by treading the soil firmly around the roots, raking the surface level and giving a good watering in.

'STOOL' PLANTS TO PROVIDE CUTTINGS

When the plants have finished flowering most of them can be discarded, but a few of each variety should be carefully labelled with name and colour, lifted and boxed or planted in a frame to provide cuttings for next year. As each 'stool' plant is capable of giving 10 to 20 good cuttings it will be seen that not many are required.

CHAPTER SIXTEEN

Dahlias for Display

THE dahlia is a magnificent display plant, for it flowers consistently, continuously and freely from mid-summer until the first real frosts of the autumn, and is available in a vast array of colours, shapes and sizes. There are brilliant colours, rich colours, delicate colours, in fact something to suit every need and taste. You can have tall dahlias for the back of a border or short dahlias for the front, with every intermediate height for use where it is required. There are spiky flowers and round flowers, shaggy flowers and smooth flowers, each type available in a whole assortment of sizes.

I like the small and medium-sized dahlias and have no room for the giant-flowered varieties—at any rate in the display garden. It is a pity that so many people, having seen these monsters at shows, seem to think of them as typical of all dahlias.

CLASSIFICATION

Because of this great diversity in dahlias and the vast numbers of varieties that have been raised, it has been necessary to devise groupings and classifications for them. A few of the names chosen for these groups could be a little misleading to the uninitiated. All the spiky-flowered kinds are called cactus or semi-cactus dahlias though they do not look remotely like any cactus. A lot of the flatter petalled types are called decoratives, and so they are, but it should not be supposed that other types are not equally decorative in the garden. The dwarf dahlias, up to about 2 ft. in height, are called bedding dahlias, but again it should not be assumed from this that they are the only ones suitable for filling beds. It just depends what you want in the bed, a short plant or a tall one.

Dahlias with globular flowers less than 2 in. in diameter are called pompons; above this size they are called ball dahlias, and can be up to 6 in. across.

You will find all these types amply described in the catalogues of nurserymen who deal in dahlias, with plenty of varieties of each from which to choose, and as nearly all dahlias today are good (they have to be or they soon get superseded by more worthy ones) you can really take your pick according to your fancy.

TROUBLES

The dahlia is a very easy plant to grow as it thrives in most soils and is not greatly troubled by pests and diseases. Aphides and capsid bugs can attack leaves and flower buds, but are easily destroyed by occasional spraying with menazon, BHC or malathion.

Left : Preparing a dahlia cutting by removing the lower leaves and trimming below a leaf joint. When rooted they are potted singly in 3-in. or 3½-in. pots. Right : Dormant dahlia tubers may be planted outside in late April or early May

Earwigs may disfigure some of the flowers, but are really more of a problem to would-be exhibitors than to display gardeners to whom an occasional faulty petal is not a major disaster. DDT powder will deal with them and with caterpillars.

The only real weakness of the dahlia is its addiction to virus diseases which weaken rather than destroy it. Most varieties contract virus of some kind after a time, but some are relatively unaffected by it. Others gradually decline and are replaced by new varieties, which partly accounts for the ever-changing names in the dahlia lists. There is not a cure for dahlia virus, so if you find a plant in your beds that is stunted, or has foliage mottled with yellow, it is best to have it out at once and burn it before the trouble is spread by aphides and capsid bugs to other plants.

PROPAGATION
Dahlias, like chrysanthemums, can be grown from cuttings taken in spring. If old plants are placed close together in

boxes in February or March, covered with any light soil or peat, placed in the greenhouse in a temperature of 13°C. to 18°C. (55°F. to 65°F.) and kept moist they will soon start to make a lot of new shoots. These can be severed, close to the parent plant, when 3 to 4 in. long and trimmed, prepared and inserted just like chrysanthemum cuttings (see p. 107). When rooted they are potted singly, again just like chrysanthemums, and soon after this are removed to a frame in which they can be given more and more ventilation until they are hardy enough, and the weather is mild enough, for them to go outdoors.

As dahlias are much more tender than chrysanthemums, this planting out will be correspondingly later; towards the end of May in the south, early in June over most of the rest of the country.

PLANTING IN THE GARDEN
Unlike chrysanthemums, dahlias do not take kindly to being moved when they are fully grown, so they must go straight into

their flowering positions. They like the soil to be rich and reasonably open. Manure or garden compost can be dug in freely before they are planted, and the surface can also be dusted with a good all-purpose fertiliser. Then the plants are carefully tapped out of their pots and planted, without root disturbance. The short varieties can be spaced 18 in. apart, the medium to tall ones 2 to 3 ft.

This is the way with dahlias grown from cuttings, but there is an alternative method which will suit those gardeners who have no glass. The dahlia has tuberous roots which can be stored in a dry, frost-proof place all the winter. These roots can be planted out of doors in late April or early May. Covered with 2 or 3 in. of soil they will be quite safe from the occasional night frosts we are likely to get during May, and by the time their shoots are through the soil the danger of frost should be over. As tubers produce more shoots than cuttings do, they should be given more space, at least 2 ft. for the dwarfs, 4 to 5 ft. for the tall ones.

Dahlias make heavier growth than chrysanthemums and it is even more brittle, so stakes must be strong and ties fairly frequent. One-inch-square wood stakes are sold for the purpose, and if treated with copper naphthanate will last for years.

Spraying, hoeing and feeding are the same as for chrysanthemums (see previous chapter). The small- and medium-flowered varieties need not be disbudded for good display, but it is necessary to look over the plants frequently to remove faded flowers which look untidy and, if they produce seed, shorten the flowering season.

STORING THE TUBERS

That is all that needs to be done until a frost arrives in autumn, sharp enough to blacken the dahlia flowers and leaves. This is the signal that the season is at an end and that it is time to cut all stems back to

Left : For cutting, side shoots of dahlias are removed but for display they are left in. Centre : Pinching out secondary buds allows the main flower to grow larger. Right : Removing faded flowers regularly, to prevent them going to seed, will help to prolong the flowering season

Growing rock plants on stone steps is another attractive way of displaying the charms of many spreading, free-flowering species and varieties. In this planting aubrieta and alyssum predominate, as happy on this plane as on a vertical wall

A dry wall provides another type of home for rock garden plants, in this case alyssum, iberis and aubrieta which are among the best plants for this purpose. The natural colour of stone allows plants of diverse colours to be used

This display is typical of the gaiety which can be created by planting dahlias, and the feast of colour is maintained from mid-summer until autumnal frosts arrive to blacken the growths. The wide range of types, shapes,

Spray chrysanthemums, which can be grown without disbudding, are available in a wide range of colours that blend well together. In this instance they have been combined effectively with decorative and cactus dahlias,

Left : The stems of dahlia plants can be cut back once the foliage has been blackened by the first hard frost. Each plant should be labelled clearly with the name of the variety. Right : Before storing the tubers for the winter they should be dusted with flowers of sulphur against moulds

within about 9 in. of soil level, tie a label to each plant, dig up the roots carefully and dry them off for a few days in some frost-proof place. The ideal is to place them upside down on the greenhouse staging, but if this is not possible they can go into a shed or a spare room. Then, when they are thoroughly dry, all remaining soil is knocked off them and the roots are packed into boxes and stored away in any place that is dry and cool but frost-proof. A cupboard is often as good a place as any, but do not pack your dahlia tubers too near the hot water cylinder or they may shrivel up before it is time to start them into growth again the following year. In any case it is wise to inspect the tubers occasionally for signs of rotting; dusting with flowers of sulphur will help to prevent moulds developing.

CHAPTER SEVENTEEN

Brightening Shady Corners

THERE are quite a number of plants that enjoy shade, so the problem of coping with such conditions is not really as difficult as many gardeners seem to imagine. I am not thinking now of a plot of poorly drained soil at the base of a high north-facing wall where no sun ever penetrates, but of a bed, say, of reasonably fertile soil that gets some sun at some period of the day. If the soil has been neglected, the first thing to do is to attempt to improve its fertility. Fork it over a week or two before planting, removing any perennial weeds, and work in some hop manure or peat which will help to retain moisture and give the plants something into which to root. Bonemeal applied at the rate of about 2 oz. to the square yard is a useful slow-acting fertiliser. Should the soil be wet and sticky fork in sharp sand, brick dust or even old sifted ashes, which will help to break up the soil and improve the drainage. If ashes are used

The aconitums are splendid plants for partially shaded positions, their 3-ft. flower spikes making an excellent show in summer. Shown below is a planting of Newry Blue, a particularly appealing variety with its flowers of dark blue

they must have weathered in the open for not less than three or four months, so do not use ashes straight from the grate. Should there be any well-rotted garden compost available this will provide valuable plant food, and it should be forked in a few inches below the surface or be used as a mulch.

HARDY PERENNIAL PLANTS FOR SHADE

Aconitum (Monkshood). Several species and varieties of aconitum thrive in moist soil and shade. The 3-ft. spikes of blue flowers in summer are delightful. The blue and white Blue Sceptre, the deep blue Newry Blue and the violet-blue Bressingham Spire are good modern hybrids.

Anemone. The Japanese anemones (varieties of *A. hybrida*, often listed erroneously as *A. japonica*), include shades of pink, rose, ruby, and white. There are double and semi-double varieties of these late summer-flowering plants which vary from 2 to 4 ft. high.

Aquilegia (Columbine). Long-spurred hybrid aquilegias are old favourites in shades of pink, crimson, purple and blue, flowering in May and June on $2\frac{1}{2}$ ft. stems. They may also be grown in full sun so long as the soil does not dry out, but the flowering season is not there so long. The 2 ft. tall Crimson Star is a charming crimson and white, free-flowering hybrid.

Astilbe. These spiraea-like plants with dainty foliage and graceful plumes of red, pink or white flowers are a joy in summer, and are more fully described in Chapter Eighteen (p. 123) as waterside plants. Splendid as they are for such conditions, they will also grow well in other moist places.

Bergenia. Useful edging plants with thick leathery leaves and short spikes of pink, red and white flowers in March and April. Height 1 ft.

Bleeding Heart (see Dicentra)

Bronze Leaf (see Rodgersia)

Brunnera. Perhaps better known as *Anchusa myosotidiflora,* the blue forget-me-

Left : The large-leaved bergenias, of which B. cordifolia *is the best known representative, are useful edging plants which provide good ground cover. Right : The blue forget-me-not-like flowers of* Brunnera macrophylla *have a graceful appearance which offset the heaviness of some other border flowers*

Left : Convallaria majalis, *the lovely fragrant Lily-of-the-Valley, is one of the joys of spring. It prefers a moist position. Right : The arching sprays of pink and white flowers and the light green fern-like foliage give* Dicentra spectabilis *unusual charm*

not-like flowers of *B. macrophylla* are borne in dainty sprays in June. Height 1 to 1½ ft.

Christmas Rose (see Helleborus)

Cimicifuga. In July and August the sprays of creamy-white flowers of *C. racemosa* are borne on 3½ ft. stems. The dainty foliage is also attractive.

Columbine (see Aquilegia)

Convallaria (Lily-of-the-Valley). A fragrant, spring-flowering plant, preferring a moist position, which should be left undisturbed for several years after planting.

Day Lily (see Hemerocallis)

Dicentra (Bleeding Heart, or Dutchman's Breeches). The handsome *D. spectabilis* bears sprays of pink and white flowers in May and June. It likes a sheltered corner where the soil is light and rich. The light green fern-like foliage is most attractive.

Digitalis (Foxglove). These seed them-

selves readily and will soon form a colony. The common foxglove is a biennial, as are the Excelsior Hybrids which have flowers all round the stem, and there are pure white foxgloves which show up well against a dark background.

Doronicum. The bright yellow *Doronicum* Harpur Crewe has been grown in gardens for many years and is full of flower in April and May. The new deep yellow, double-flowered Spring Beauty flowers early on 18-in. stems, which are shorter than those of some of the other varieties.

Dutchman's Breeches (see Dicentra)

Epimedium. An attractive genus of plants with handsome foliage which turns a pleasing bronze and remains on the plant throughout the winter. *E. versicolor sulphureum* is the one most often grown and it bears its pale sulphur-yellow flowers in spring on 9-in. stems. It is useful for suppressing weeds.

Foam Flower (see Tiarella)

Left : The flowers of the Christmas Rose, Helleborus niger, *are with us from Christmas to March. The white flowers should be protected with a cloche in severe weather. Right :* Kirengeshoma palmata *combines very decorative lobed leaves with pale yellow flowers which are borne in autumn*

Foxglove (see Digitalis)

Gentiana. The Willow Gentian, *G. asclepiadea,* has arching, 18-in. stems, bearing dark blue flowers in July and August. It likes a moist, leafy soil. There is also a white form.

Helleborus. The Christmas Rose, *H. niger,* and the Lenten Rose, *H. orientalis,* as well as other species and varieties, thrive in shade and in a moist but well-drained soil. The long-lasting flowers, particularly of the Christmas Rose, should be protected with a cloche in stormy weather, for otherwise the blooms may be spoiled.

Hemerocallis (Day Lily). Day Lilies do best in a fairly moist soil, and they are described in Chapter Five (p. 40).

Hosta (Plantain Lily). These are one of the best plants for fairly moist shade. They are described in Chapter Eighteen (pp. 124, 129).

Kirengeshoma. The Japanese *K. palmata*

bears charming tubular, drooping yellow flowers in the autumn on stems about 3 ft. high. The large, lobed leaves are also attractive for much of the year. It likes a moist, leafy soil.

Lenten Rose (see Helleborus)

Lily-of-the-Valley (see Convallaria)

Mertensia. The Virginian Cowslip, *M. virginica,* bears pendulous, blue, bell-shaped flowers on arching stems in May. The glaucous leaves are also attractive while they last. It grows up to 2 ft. tall and requires plenty of moisture during the growing season.

Monkshood (see Aconitum)

Navel Wort (see Omphalodes)

Omphalodes (Navel Wort). The sprays of deep blue forget-me-not-like flowers of *O. cappadocica* are borne on stems up to 9 in. high in May and June. It does best in a moist, well-drained soil and in light shade.

Plantain Lily (see Hosta)

[121]

Left : The Solomon's Seal, Polygonatum multiflorum, *which bears white bell-like flowers on gracefully arched stems. Right : The bold, handsome leaves and pinkish flower plumes of* Rodgersia aesculifolia *make this plant stand out in any company*

Polygonatum (Solomon's Seal). With its clusters of pendulous white bells the Solomon's Seal makes a graceful plant. These flowers are borne on arching stems up to $2\frac{1}{2}$ ft. long in June.

Rodgersia (Bronze Leaf). These handsome plants take some little time to become established but are well worth growing. The leaves of *R. aesculifolia* are similar to those of the Horse Chestnut, and plumes of fragrant, pinkish flowers appear in July. Height 3 ft.

Solomon's Seal (see Polygonatum)

Tiarella (Foam Flower). The common name aptly describes *T. cordifolia*, for it bears little spikes of creamy-white flowers, pink in the bud stage, on 9-in. stems from May to July. The heart-shaped leaves are also attractive and colourful in the autumn.

Trillium (Wood Lily). For moist woodland, trilliums are excellent, and are described in Chapter Eighteen (p. 132).

Virginian Cowslip (see Mertensia)

Wood Lily (see Trillium)

Waterside Plants for Colour

MANY waterside or bog plants are most colourful, and if thought is given to their siting, remarkably beautiful effects may be achieved by reflections in the water, particularly that of a placid pool. But the colour should not be overdone, or it will destroy the cool restfulness one associates with water in the garden. The feathery heads of pink, crimson or white astilbes standing above the mass of handsome green foliage will be doubly effective when seen across a pool, and the elegant heads of the Japanese *Iris kaempferi* are serenely beautiful when growing beside water. Generally speaking, planting is best done in early spring and the finest effect is produced with bold clumps of one variety, rather than dotting odd specimens here and there. The number in each group will, of course, depend upon the size of the pool or the length of the stream.

HARDY WATERSIDE PLANTS

Astilbe. These graceful plants are often confused with spiraeas. They thrive in moist soil beside and above water-level in sun or partial shade. Among the popular named varieties are Fanal, garnet red; Granat, dark crimson; Rheinland, clear pink, and Deutschland, probably the best white. Their flower spikes are about $2\frac{1}{2}$ to 3 ft. in height, and the main period of flowering is in July and August. An imposing tall Chinese species is *A. davidii*, with long spikes of rose-lavender flowers in July and August from 4 to 6 ft. high. There are also dwarf species for a cool, moist corner on the rock garden, such as *A. glaberrima saxosa* with rosy-pink plumes which it bears on 4-in. stems in late summer.

Caltha (Marsh Marigold or Kingcup). One of the earliest plants to flower in the water garden, *C. palustris* bears rich golden flowers on 12-in. stems and the leaves are dark green and glossy. There are various forms including a fine double variety with long-lasting flowers, *C. p. flore pleno*.

Day Lily (see Hemerocallis)

Giant Cow Parsnip (see Heracleum)

Globe Flower (see Trollius)

Hemerocallis (Day Lily). Day Lilies have been much improved in recent years and there are now some hybrids with very attractive colouring to plant in a moist, wild garden. The colour range is from pale yellow to mahogany-crimson. They associate well with astilbes, hostas and the like. Flowering over a long period from June

The showy double Marsh Marigold, Caltha palustris flore pleno, *is one of the earliest flowering waterside plants and its golden flowers and dark green, glossy foliage are a lovely sight, especially when reflected in still water*

to September, they are in their full glory in July and August. Most are $2\frac{1}{2}$ to $3\frac{1}{2}$ ft. tall.

Heracleum. Given sufficient space, the Giant Cow Parsnip, *H. mantegazzianum,* with its large leaves and large flat heads of white flowers in summer is a plant to pro-vide interest in the middle distance of streamside plantings. But it is 10 ft. tall and is nearly as much across so only suitable for spacious settings. Also, if well suited, it can seed itself freely—so use with dis-cretion.

Hosta (Plantain Lily). These are admirable

Left : Stream-side plantings should always be made with an eye to form as well as colour, and the Giant Cow Parsnip, Heracleum mantegazzianum, *will provide interest where the scale is appropriate. Right : Hostas, with their highly ornamental leaves, find waterside conditions much to their liking*

Aquilegias, or Columbines to give them their lovely common name, are almost everybody's favourites with their delicate habit and soft colourings. For providing a May-June display in a shady position the long-spurred hybrids are an excellent choice, and they may also be grown in sun, as long as the soil is not allowed to dry out

The azaleas in this woodland setting are an example of the art of balancing 'hot' colours against the more sombre colours which must inevitably be present in dappled shade. Scale and proportion must, in such instances, be assessed with an artist's intuition

[125]

Given the conditions they like, moisture-living primulas of many kinds seed themselves freely and soon form colourful colonies which add much to the garden scene. Primula bulleyana and others growing in the author's Shropshire garden, have all the lush beauty one associates with the genus

A formal or informal pool, stream or other water feature will, if well sited or landscaped as the case may be, enhance the beauty of a garden to an extraordinary degree. This informal pool with its still water has ideal partners in the graceful astilbes which fringe its banks and the overhanging willow

[126]

Above: For modern homes with paved areas or patios there is a whole world of delight to be gained by growing plants in containers. Hydrangeas, geraniums, lobelias, fuchsias—these and numerous others can be grown to provide a display spanning many months. Below Left: Near-white concrete urns with their rather severe shape are admirably suited for the display of these ivy-leaved geraniums, trailing lobelia, lantana and heliotrope. Below Right: A stone sink planted with a dwarf conifer, mat-forming and other very small alpine plants

In this border grey-foliaged plants such as Stachys lanata and santolina have been used successfully as a foil for the other colours. The colour scheme overall, with its emphasis on pastel shades, is especially pleasing to the eye. Note how the colours of the lupins and linums are enhanced

This lovely study in pastel shades, in Mrs Margery Fish's well known garden at East Lambrook Manor, South Petherton, Somerset, is a forceful reminder that garden beauty in its purest form owes less to strong colours than most of us realise. The allium and Anaphalis triplinervis in the fore-ground, the helichrysums and the glaucous green Euphorbia wulfenii by

The Japanese Iris kaempferi *is a popular plant for waterside planting. The flowers, which include colours from purple and violet to lavender and white, are borne freely in July on 2-ft. stems*

for planting near water where their large, prominently veined, cool-looking leaves are most effective. There are many different species and varieties, some with glaucous, others with variegated, foliage. They include *H. undulata* with green and white leaves and *H. fortunei* with glaucous-green leaves. Once planted they should be left undisturbed to form large clumps. The funnel-shaped flowers are borne on stems from 1 to 3 ft. in height and are in shades of lilac, mauve, pale purple and white. They like partial shade although they will flourish in sun so long as the soil, which should be rich, does not dry out.

Iris. A very large genus, some of which are waterside plants. Among the better known are the Japanese *I. kaempferi* with elegant flat heads of velvety flowers in shades of violet, purple, plum, yellow and white, borne in July on erect stems 2 ft. or more in height. They require a lime-free soil, as does the rich blue *I. laevigata* which will grow in water about 3 in. deep, or on the water's edge where its roots can go down below water level. The dainty *I. sibirica* is a delight in June with its bluish-purple flowers on slender 3-ft. stems. There are several good named hybrids, the flowers of Perry's Blue being a most attractive sky-blue colour with a touch of white on the falls, while Caesar is a large, violet-purple. Where space permits the Yellow Flag, *Iris pseudacorus,* is worth planting in shallow water or on the brink of water. This is the iris that may be seen growing wild in ponds and ditches. The flowers open one at a time and continue throughout May and June on stems up to about 3 ft. high.

Kingcup (see Caltha)

Lysichitum (Skunk Cabbage). The yellow-flowered *L. americanum* has most striking arum-like flowers which it bears in April and these are followed by enormous deep

Left : The common name of Lysichitum americanum, *Skunk Cabbage, refers to its unpleasant odour and the very large leaves, but it is grown of course for the yellow, arum-like flowers. Right : The gay trumpet-like flowers of mimulus hybrids which are borne in profusion throughout the summer*

green leaves. The flowers have a foul smell and should never be cut for use indoors. It is perfectly hardy and revels in thick mud at the water's edge. There is also a white species, *L. camtschatcense,* which flowers a few weeks later. Both are plants for a large garden.

Marsh Marigold (see Caltha)

Mimulus (Musk). These gay moisture-loving plants produce a profusion of flower throughout the summer. There are numerous species and varieties, both perennial and annual, the latter being easily raised

The Bartley Strain of Primula pulverulenta *is especially beautiful with its flowers in shades of pink, salmon, apricot and buff. These appear during June and July and are borne on stems 2 to 3 ft. tall*

The Wake Robin, Trillium grandiflorum, *is a choice plant for a position near, but above, the water. The white flowers are a delight in spring and have an appropriate foil in the handsome foliage*

from seed sown in damp soil at the water's edge. The markings on the little trumpet-like flowers in shades of orange, yellow, red and pink are delightful, and there are self-coloured varieties.

Musk (see Mimulus)

Osmunda. The Royal Fern, *Osmunda regalis,* is a magnificent spectacle with its large, handsome fronds, perhaps 4 ft. in length, swaying beside a pool. When planted on a small mound surrounded by boggy soil it thrives luxuriantly. Planting is best done in the spring just when growth starts. It will grow in partial shade or in sun so long as the roots have adequate moisture.

Plantain Lily (see Hosta)

Primula. A very large genus, many of which thrive in bog gardens. Once established some of the varieties will seed themselves happily and soon form colourful colonies. They like moisture at the roots but should not be 'stuck in the mud'. One

of the earliest to flower, in April, is *Primula rosea,* with bright pink flowers on 6-in. stems above tufts of pale green leaves. This is a real bog plant. Earlier still is *P. denticulata.* This species, with its globular, mauve flowers, and its white form, *alba,* do not require so much moisture to sustain their 12-inch stems. The flowers of this primula appear from March to May. Growing taller, up to 18 in., *P. beesiana,* with fragrant rosy-carmine flower heads, and *P. bulleyana,* pale orange, are a delight from May onwards. These and *P. florindae* often seed themselves with abandon. The soft yellow, drooping flowers of *P. florindae* are carried on 3-ft. stems in July and August. It will grow in sun or partial shade given plenty of moisture. Other bright species are *P. japonica* with tiers of pink, crimson or white flowers on 2-ft. stems, and *P. pulverulenta,* which is similar but taller, and the whorls of flower are crimson. There are many beautiful hybrids known as the Bartley Strain in shades of pink, salmon, apricot and buff.

[131]

The Globe Flower, Trollius europaeus, *bears distinctive pale yellow, globe-like flowers and has attractive deeply divided foliage. Some excellent hybrids are available in shades of yellow and orange*

Royal Fern (see Osmunda)

Skunk Cabbage (see Lysichitum)

Trillium (Wood Lily). These spring-flowering woodland plants do well in partial shade and moist soil near, but above, the water. They like a rich leafy soil and once planted should be left undisturbed. *T. grandiflorum,* the Wake Robin, has large pure white three-petalled flowers and there are other North American species, some of which are still rare in cultivation.

Trollius (Globe Flower). *T. europaeus* has large globe-shaped pale yellow flowers on 18-in. stems from May onwards and there are some splendid hybrids—Canary Bird, soft yellow; Golden Monarch, a large, rich yellow, and Orange Princess, among others. Given plenty of moisture at the roots they will present no difficulty in cultivation.

Wake Robin (see Trillium)

Wood Lily (see Trillium)

CHAPTER NINETEEN

Single Colour Borders
White

WHERE space permits effects of great beauty can be achieved by planting a hardy perennial border with a variety of different plants all of one colour, or shades of one colour. For instance, a border consisting entirely of white flowers can be most striking, particularly if there is a dark evergreen hedge, such as yew, in the background. Some might consider that it would be monotonous, but in fact it can be unusually beautiful.

Depending upon the individual garden, such a border could be in the shape of a half moon, or an island bed; or, if there is no alternative, just a straight bed beside a path with a hedge, wall or fence as a background.

Taller Plants

For such a border, or for an island bed so long as it is not too exposed, plant stately white delphiniums, white hollyhocks, the tall white Mugwort, *Artemisia lactiflora* (5 ft.), the branching *Asphodelus cerasiferus* (4 to 5 ft.), and, nearer the front of the bed, *A. albus* (2 ft.), with clusters of bell-shaped flowers. The milky coloured Bell-flower, *Campanula lactiflora alba,* has an erect stem about 4 ft. in height and will grow in sun or partial shade. The creamy-white *Cimicifuga racemosa* has graceful feathery sprays of white flowers on stems up to 5 or 6 ft. in July and August. The flowers droop elegantly and this is a most useful plant for a moist soil in partial shade.

Where space permits, the spreading *Crambe cordifolia,* with its huge rounded leaves and 5-ft. flower spikes with branching panicles of little white flowers is quite effective. The flowers appear in June and July. One plant is usually sufficient unless the border is extensive. Although biennial, pure white foxgloves grouped together have attractive spikes about 4 to 5 ft. high. They are easily raised from seed sown in the open from May to July. They are listed in seed catalogues under *Digitalis*.

The handsome *Filipendula camtschatica* produces in July large plumes of fragrant fleecy white flowers on stems that may reach 8 ft. in height. It is a magnificent plant, with its imposing palmate leaves, for a moist place or beside a pool. Taller than the common Solomon's Seal, *Polygonatum commutatum* has large white flowers on stems up to 6 ft. The common Solomon's Seal (*P. multiflorum*) does not usually exceed $2\frac{1}{2}$ ft., but its arching stems in June bearing small white bells are most pleasing in a shaded, moist place.

Where height is an advantage Filipendula camtschatica, *up to 8 ft. tall, can be a very useful plant. The fleecy white flowers are carried in July above handsome palmate leaves*

The Sorrel Rhubarb, *Rheum palmatum,* should only be planted where there is ample space to fill, or as a specimen plant. It has handsome, spreading, five-lobed leaves and cream-coloured flowers on 5-ft. stems in June and July. It requires a deep, rich soil and flourishes in sun or partial shade.

Flowering from July until September, the huge white fragrant flowers of *Romneya coulteri* are borne on erect stems up to 6 ft. in height. It likes a well-drained sunny position and in colder districts this native of California should have its roots protected with old ashes or bracken. It dies down to the ground each autumn, but makes rapid growth in the spring. Similar, but rather less tall is *R. trichocalyx.* Once these have been planted they should be left undisturbed for years. They are not easy to establish, but are well worth a little trouble.

The stately veratrum has striking, deeply ribbed leaves and does best in partial shade and a porous soil containing some peat or leafmould. The species *V. album* grows from 4 to 5 ft. high, bearing branching pyramids of flowers which are green outside and white when fully open. The flowering season extends from July to September.

Plants of Lesser Stature

When we come to consider plants of lesser stature the choice is almost embarrassing. Such plants are, of course, more suitable for windy gardens or for island beds set in a lawn.

The anaphalis, or Pearl Everlasting, of which there are several varying in height from 1 to 2 ft., have dense woolly silver-grey leaves and white flowers in late summer. They like a gravelly soil and sun, and are popular these days for decorative arrangements, even when cut and dried for winter use. The fern-like aromatic leaves, silvery-grey in colour, of *Anthemis cupaniana,* form a spreading plant which bears large white daisy-like flowers throughout the summer. It presents no difficulty when grown in well-drained soil and in a sunny position. Among the many Michaelmas daisies or asters, Mount Everest (4 ft.) is a good white and Snow Sprite (1 ft.) is one of the best dwarfs. For a cool moist place, or by the side of a pool so that one gets a charming reflection in the water few plants are as beautiful as the astilbes— White Queen is a good variety.

Lily-of-the-Valley is, of course, a charming, low-growing, deliciously fragrant plant for a moist, partially shady place with a leafy soil. Once planted the crowns should be left undisturbed for years. Our old friend Mrs Sinkins is one of the hardiest of the pinks and thrives in full sun and in well-drained soil. The old lady is fragrant too. This is but one of the many good white dianthus and border carnations which are so delightful in the summer months. Gypsophila, for some unknown reason, seems to be out of favour, yet it is a trouble-free plant, perfectly hardy, and produces a mass of feathery little white flowers for

many weeks during the summer. It does particularly well on chalky soil.

Then there are white peonies, lupins, poppies, phlox, scabious, thalictrum, thrift (*Armeria maritima alba*) for the very front of a border, heuchera, and the ivory-white *Kniphofia* Maid of Orleans, an elegant member of the Red Hot Poker family, which bears its spikes of flower on $3\frac{1}{2}$-ft. stems for an exceptionally long time throughout the summer.

The trilliums, such as the Wake Robin, *T. grandiflorum,* have handsome foliage as well as enchanting flowers in the spring when planted in moist, leafy soil and in partial shade. And do not forget the primula family which has its white-flowered forms, such as the easily grown *P. denticulata alba* which brings forth its drumstick heads of white flowers from March until May on stems up to 1 ft. in height. These and other primulas like plenty of moisture.

A selection from the plants I have mentioned should provide a succession of white flowers in the border from the spring until the autumn.

Gypsophila paniculata *Bristol Fairy is a trouble-free border plant which makes an effective display with a profusion of small, white double flowers*

CHAPTER TWENTY

Single Colour Borders
Blue

BLUE seems to be a particularly popular colour, especially with the ladies, although of course fashions change remarkably quickly. So far as the garden is concerned a blue border, ranging through all the finer shades, and including mauve and violet, can be a most delightful and restful feature from early summer until the autumn. In a town garden one can have small island beds of shorter-growing plants in a sunny position, or a border with a background of a wall, fence or hedge, to protect taller growing plants from damage by summer gales which can be troublesome.

If one includes hardy annuals with herbaceous perennials the choice is very wide. I shall first consider perennials and then add a few suitable blue annuals to fill in any unexpected gaps, for even in the best-planned garden gaps do appear, for reasons sometimes unaccountable.

Taller Plants

Among the taller plants suitable for the back of a border, or for the middle of an island bed in a lawn where it is not too exposed to summer gales, there is a wide choice of delphiniums in shades of lavender, lilac, deep blue, light blue, silvery-blue, gentian blue and so on. Many will produce elegant spikes 6 ft. or more in height, and there are shorter-growing varieties more suitable for windy gardens. One of the neatest is the brilliant, medium blue Pageboy with a white eye (3 ft.). Planting unnamed delphiniums raised from seed saved from named varieties is an economical way of buying plants where a quantity is required.

Anchusas are indispensable plants for a sunny border where the soil is well drained. There are various named varieties with intense blue spikes of flower—Opal, light blue, and Morning Glory, bright blue, which are both about 5 ft. in height; and the 3 ft. tall gentian blue Loddon Royalist which is an excellent variety with erect heads of large flowers in late May and throughout June.

There is such a galaxy of colour in modern lupins that a mere blue spike is not looked upon with much interest these days, which is a pity because they are very beautiful. Tree lupins, such as Mauve Queen, rapidly make bushy plants up to 5 ft. in height.

The only way to perpetuate a good variety is by cuttings taken in March. The lupin has been hybridised to such an extent that seedlings will not come true to

The blue teazle-like flower heads of the eryngiums or Sea Hollies, surrounded by ruffs of stiff bracts, are well worth growing for their colour and form. Shown above is Eryngium alpinum *Amethyst, 2½ ft. tall. The Sea Hollies need a well-drained soil and sunny position*

colour, although one may produce some good colours from a batch of seed saved from selected plants.

The shrubby *Perovskia atriplicifolia* is most attractive in August and September with its erect spikes of soft blue flowers which may attain a height of about 4 ft. It likes a sunny position and a well-drained soil. The leaves are silvery-grey and the whole plant has a sage-like aroma. A group of, say, three plants in a largish border, would be most effective. Each plant should be allowed about 3 square feet of space.

The dainty thalictrums or Meadow Rue, with their fern-like foliage and graceful sprays of mauve flowers, make a charming feature in a border. They like adequate moisture at the roots but also need good drainage, and being fast growing they like a rich root run. The soft purple *T. aquilegifolium* flowers in May and June with stems up to 3 ft. in height, and *T. dipterocarpum*

flowers from June into August with rosy-mauve panicles up to 5 ft. high. The rich mauve Hewitt's Double is a striking form. For a similar soil, but in partial shade, the Willow Gentian, *Gentiana asclepiadea,* with arching sprays of tubular, dark blue flowers, is an interesting plant for near the front of the border.

Then there are mauve phlox and Michaelmas daisies; so far as the latter are concerned there are some tall and some dwarf varieties to suit both the back and the front of a border.

The most useful late-flowering *Vernonia crinita* has erect stems up to 6 ft. or more bearing flat heads of purplish flowers well into late autumn. It can be grouped with Michaelmas daisies, flowering as it does at the same period.

Less-tall Plants

Among blue-flowered plants of lesser

[137]

Perovskia atriplicifolia is a 4 ft.-tall shrub which combines soft blue flower spikes with silvery-grey foliage. Planted in a border or on top of a retaining wall it can be a considerable attraction when flowering in August and September

stature are aconitum (Monkshood); agapanthus, such as the Headbourne Hybrids which have proved quite hardy in many gardens in southern England; aquilegias, campanulas, the long-lasting *Catananche caerulea,* and the Globe Thistle, *Echinops ritro,* whose metallic blue heads are also long lasting. The Sea Holly, or eryngium, is also thistle like and the deep blue teazle-shaped heads may be cut and dried for winter use. There are blue erigerons, hardy geraniums, such as our native blue Meadow

Left : A lovely blue-flowered plant for moist, partially shaded places is the Tibetan Blue Poppy, Meconopsis betonicifolia, which flowers in May and June. Right : The much-loved hardy annual nigella, or Love-in-a-Mist, is a charming blue-flowered plant. The colour range of this flower also includes pink, rose, purple and mauve

Cranesbill, *G. pratense,* which flowers so freely during the summer; flag irises, in many beautiful shades and with a honeyed fragrance; nepeta (catmint), blue polyanthus and primulas, and a very old favourite, the Pincushion Flower or scabious. Sea Lavender (limonium, better known as statice) is also a popular perennial plant of which there are several named varieties well worth growing.

For a moist, partially shaded place two plants that must not be forgotten are the Tibetan Blue Poppy, *Meconopsis betonicifolia,* and the Virginian Cowslip, *Mertensia virginica,* with drooping heads of blue bells in May and early June. The meconopsis can prove temperamental, but given a cool, peaty acid soil it should be quite happy. It is as well not to let the plants flower the first year or they may disappear. Pinch out the flower stem when quite young and the plants should then form several crowns to produce flowers the following year.

Some Annuals

The first year after planting a perennial border it may well be that hardy annuals will prove most useful to provide additional colour until the permanent plants have become thoroughly established. There is no shortage of blue and lavender-coloured annuals which may be used for this purpose, and they may be sown in the open, where they are to flower (for sowing instructions see p. 29).

Some hardy annuals may be sown in the open in the autumn to flower earlier than spring sowings. Among these are Larkspur, Cornflower, Love-in-a-Mist, such as *Nigella* Miss Jekyll, sky blue, and Oxford Blue; Sweet Scabious, and the Candytuft *Iberis* Lilac Queen. If further sowings of these are made in the spring then the display will be considerably extended.

Blue-flowering hardy annuals for spring sowing include *Anchusa* Blue Bird, asperula, cynoglossum, *Echium* Blue Bedder, gilia, and *Salvia farinacea* Blue Bedder.

CHAPTER TWENTY-ONE

Studies in Grey

SILVER-FOLIAGED herbaceous and shrubby plants, carefully sited in a garden, paying special attention to their background, can be most effective over a long period. Generally speaking these plants like a sunny position and a well-drained soil, and growing in the sun they stand out in all their beauty against a background of evergreens or, failing this, tall herbaceous plants with large green leaves. They will also show up well in the sun against a dark wooded fence.

Where something fairly bold is required, *Senecio laxifolius* will make a handsome shrub of about 3 ft. in height, broadly spreading in habit and perhaps 6 ft. wide. It is evergrey, and in the summer has many sprays of yellow daisy-like flowers. Sprigs of this plant are most effective when used in floral decorations, particularly with dianthus or pinks which associate so happily with grey-foliaged plants.

The Lavender Cotton, *Santolina incana*, also has yellow flowers, in this case little buttons, and the silvery-grey foliage is aromatic. It makes a neat little bush about 18 in. high. There is a more compact form, known as *nana*, which hardly reaches 12 in. The velvety texture of Lamb's Ear, or *Stachys lanata*, is delightful and it makes an excellent edging plant. Prostrate in

habit, it suppresses weeds. The spikes of crimson flowers are almost covered in grey wool and are at their best in July and August. It presents no problems so far as soil is concerned, but prefers a dryish position. It is easily increased by division or by seed.

The silvery *Anaphalis triplinervis* thrives in sun or dry shade and makes a compact plant with densely woolly, silver-grey leaves and bunches of off-white little flowers on 15-in. stems. The stems may be cut and will last well when dried.

There are several attractive artemisias, some with aromatic foliage. It is the foliage rather than the flowers that is effective. With stems up to about 4 ft. high, *Artemisia ludoviciana*, with its woolly white foliage, is a useful plant towards the back of the border or for cutting and using in large arrangements. About half that height is *A. nutans* with feathery silver spikes, and Silver Queen is another pleasing variety with stems about 2½ ft. high.

Where the soil is poor and dry, plant the artemisia which is commonly called Dusty Miller, *A. stelleriana*, which has finely cut silvery foliage and small yellow flowers on stems about 1 ft. in height. It has become naturalised on sandy soil in parts of south-west England.

Left : The 1-ft.-tall Artemisia stellariana *is a handsome herbaceous plant with distinctive silvery, finely cut foliage. It bears small yellow flowers in summer. Right : The 3-ft.-tall Jerusalem Sage,* Phlomis fruticosa, *has woolly leaves and bears rusty-yellow flowers in summer. It needs a well-drained soil and sunshine*

The spiky foliage or 'grass' of the dianthus family is pleasing even in the winter months, and such old friends as Mrs Sinkins, among many others, will clothe the ground with silvery-grey. Then in June and July there is the spicy fragrance of the charming blooms. The smaller alpine pinks are delightful for the rock garden, and *Alyssum saxatile* makes a bold display with its heads of bright yellow flowers and its grey leaves in early May. The variety *citrinum* has fluffy heads of pale lemon-yellow.

Also for a sunny, really dry place on a rock garden the trailing *Antirrhinum asarina* is effective, with grey leaves and ivory-yellow flowers with a yellow throat. A native of Southern France, it does not like winter wet, but is worth taking a little trouble to cultivate.

Then there is lavender, catmint (*Nepeta faassenii*, better known as *N. mussinii*) and *Gypsophila paniculata*, or Baby's Breath, which makes a great mound of grey in the summer covered with a host of tiny white flowers. When cut it is charming with a vase of sweet peas, and if used with gladioli it covers the rigid stems and makes the whole effect lighter.

In late summer the silvery-grey *Perovskia atriplicifolia,* with its slender spikes of soft blue flowers, is most decorative. The stems are erect and about 4 ft. high. This shrub is commonly called Russian Sage and likes a sunny place and a well-drained soil. Planted on top of a retaining wall it is quite outstanding. Also belonging to the sage family is the shrub *Phlomis fruticosa,* or Jerusalem Sage, which has woolly leaves and rusty-yellow flowers. These last are borne in summer on 3-ft. stems.

Among the most glorious grey-foliaged plants are the romneyas. They are not easy to get established but once they have rooted into a light, warm, well-drained soil which is to their liking, they show their approval by a magnificent display of large flowers from July to September every year. One

In gardens where they find conditions congenial—they need a light, warm well-drained soil and sunshine— the romneyas or Californian Tree Poppies make a fine display from July to September. Seen above is a planting of Romneya coulteri *with blue-grey leaves and handsome white flowers*

of the two species is *Romneya coulteri*, the Californian Tree Poppy, which is the one that is more often grown, with blue-grey leaves and satiny white flowers about 4 in. across with a conspicuous mass of golden stamens. Very similar, *R. trichocalyx* is less branching and not so tall. Once planted, romneyas should be left undisturbed and they will spread by means of underground roots.

There is a strange little Australian shrub known as *Calocephalus brownii*, or Cushion Bush, which is suitable for growing in a frost-free greenhouse. It forms a rigid plant about 1 ft. high, densely covered with silvery-grey foliage. It is useful in summer for window boxes or for planting out in front of a border, but must be lifted and given protection during the winter or it will not survive.

CHAPTER TWENTY-TWO

Plants in Containers

PLANT containers such as window boxes, balcony boxes, tubs, hanging baskets and the like will bring colour where space is restricted, or for that matter to a terrace, patio or roof garden. So far as window boxes are concerned the size is naturally controlled by the dimensions of the sill upon which it is to stand. It should not be less than 6 in. deep and as broad as is feasible, for the smaller the box the quicker it will dry out during hot weather, and that means more watering. All sorts of boxes are available, hardwood, rustic elm, and teak as well, lightweight polystyrene troughs, in different sizes and in a wide range of prices.

Any such container must have drainage holes in the bottom, for otherwise the soil will become sour. Most boxes and tubs made for this purpose have such holes, but it is as well to make sure. The holes must be covered with broken pieces of flower pot, commonly called 'crocks', placed hollow side downwards over the holes to prevent them from becoming clogged with soil. Over these should be spread a thin layer of small pebbles or moss litter to a depth of about 1 in. If the box is large and deep enough, old pieces of turf placed grass side downwards will provide more nourishment and moisture for the plant's roots.

THE SOIL MIXTURE

This brings me to the all-important question of soil which may not be an easy matter for flat dwellers, and those with town houses. It is a waste of time to fill boxes with poor, infertile soil dug from some corner of a town garden. The simplest way is to buy a bag of John Innes potting compost, sufficient for your needs, or where there are the facilities for preparing a compost use the following: 3 parts good loam, 2 parts well-rooted leafmould or granulated peat, and 1 part sharp silver sand (all parts by volume). A liberal handful of bonemeal should be added to each bushel of soil. This is a slow-acting fertiliser which will become available to the plants as they mature.

The container should be filled to within about an inch of the top, and the soil pressed firmly but gently to ensure that the corners and space along the sides are well filled. The soil should, of course, be moist but not wet.

Hanging Baskets

Stout wire hanging baskets are usually suspended by three chains or wires from a

Left : Good drainage is particularly important when plants are grown in a window box. There must be drainage holes in the bottom of the box and these should be covered with a layer of 'crocks'. Right : The compost used should come to within about an inch of the top, leaving adequate room for watering

hook. Be sure that such a hook is firmly fixed, because a basket filled with soil and plants is surprisingly heavy. The basket is lined with fresh, damp moss which must be laid thickly enough to retain the soil within the basket. Use sturdy plants, pre-ferably pot grown, and water them well an hour or so before putting them into the basket. Knock the plants out of the pots, remove the crock from the bottom of the ball of soil, and, if the plant is well-rooted, loosen the roots gently to assist them to

Left : For a spring display there is nothing quite so pleasing as a batch of well-grown daffodils. Right : Geraniums (pelargoniums) are also superb window box subjects, providing a display from June to September

A balcony provides opportunities to grow a colourful display of plants in window boxes and other containers. Geraniums and marguerites are being grown in the display shown above.

grow quickly into the new compost. A medium-sized basket will take three plants that have been grown in 5-in. pots, and probably three or more that have been grown in 3½-in. pots. Where young plants of trailing lobelia are used, these can be placed hanging downwards by pushing the ball of roots up into the basket between the wires and then firmly pressing the moss and soil around the roots. Ivy-leaved geraniums are very suitable for planting in the top to trail over the sides.

Selecting Plants

When buying plants, particularly those grown in boxes, avoid those that are 'leggy' or starved and with yellowing leaves. Choose young, bushy plants with healthy green foliage—the others are not cheap at any price.

SPRING-FLOWERING PLANTS

Many of these can be bought in bud or in bloom in the early spring ready for planting out in window boxes and tubs.

Bellis perennis (Button Daisy), pink, red and white. 6 in., April.

Cheiranthus allionii (Siberian Wallflower), orange. 9 to 12 in., April and May.

Myosotis (Forget-me-Not). Royal Blue is an outstanding variety. 8 in., May.

Pansies, various beautiful colours. 6 in., April, May onwards.

Polyanthuses, many bright colours. 8 in., April and May.

Primula E. R. Janes, rose-pink. 3 in., March.

Primula Wanda, rich purple-crimson. 4 in., March.

Stocks, East Lothian, many beautiful colours. Fragrant. 12 to 18 in., May.

Stocks, Brompton, a fine range of colours. 1 to 2 ft., May.

SUMMER-FLOWERING PLANTS

Many of these can be bought as small plants ready for planting out in containers in mid-May:

Ageratum Imperial Dwarf Blue. 9 in., July to September.

Antirrhinum nanum, various colours. 15 in., July to September.

Begonias, red, orange, pink and white. 8 to 12 in., July to October.

Calceolarias (dwarf varieties), yellow and brown. 12 in. June to October.

Calendulas (Marigold), yellow and orange. 12 to 18 in., May to September.

Celosias (Cockscombs), red and yellow. 18 in. summer.

Centaurea (Cornflower), blue and pink. 12 in., June to August.

Chrysanthemums (annual varieties), various colours. 1 to 3 ft., July to September.

Convolvulus major, blue, pink and white. 12 in., July to September.

Dahlias (dwarf bedding), various colours. 12 to 18 in., July to October.

Fuchsias, pink, rose and purple. 1 to 2 ft., July to September.

Heliotropes (Cherry Pie), mauve and purple. 12 to 18 in., June to September.

Hydrangeas, crimson, pink and blue. 1 to 3 ft., summer.

Lobelias, blue and white. 12 in. (and trailing varieties), June to October.

Marguerites, white and yellow. 1 to 2 ft., June to October.

Nasturtium, golden, yellow, scarlet and maroon. 6 to 12 in. (and trailing), July to October.

Pansies, various bright colours. 6 in., May to September.

Pelargoniums (Geraniums), many colours. 12 to 18 in., June to September.

Penstemons, various colours. 1 to 2 ft., June to September.

Petunias, various bright colours. 6 to 12 in., June to September.

Phlox drummondii (dwarf), crimson, pink, purple and white. 6 to 9 in., July to October.

Stocks, Ten-week, various colours. 15 to 18 in., July to August.

Tagetes (African Marigold), bright yellow. 12 in., July to October.

Ursinias, bright orange. 9 to 12 in., June to July.

Violas, mauve, purple and white. 6 to 9 in., May to July.

BULBOUS PLANTS

Chionodoxas (Glory of the Snow), rich blue. March.

Crocuses, purple, yellow and white. March.

Daffodils, golden-yellow. March and April.

Hyacinths, in variety. April.

Iris reticulata, rich violet. February and March.

Muscari (Grape Hyacinth), sky-blue. April.

Scillas (Dwarf Squills), deep blue. March.

Snowdrops, white. February.

Tulips (Double and Early Single varieties). April.

Index